BOHEMIAN MODERN

BOHEMIAN MODERN
LIVING IN SILVER LAKE

Barbara Bestor
Drawings by Geoff McFetridge

ReganBooks
An Imprint of HarperCollinsPublishers

Bohemian Modern
Living in Silver Lake
Barbara Bestor
with Kimberly Stevens

Photographs by Joshua White
Drawings by Geoff McFetridge
Portraits by Jon Huck
Additional art and photograph credits on page 261.

HarperCollins books may be purchased for educational,
business, or sales promotional use. For information
please write: Special Markets Department, HarperCollins
Publishers Inc., 10 East 53rd Street, New York,
NY 10022.

First edition

Designed by Michael Worthington & Eli Carrico
with Yasmin Khan and Jiwon Lee

Printed on acid-free paper

Library of Congress Cataloging-in-Publication Data
has been applied for.

ISBN 0-06-079215-9
06 07 08 09 10 TP 10 9 8 7 6 5 4 3 2 1

For Beatrice and Charlotte

contents

07 ECHO PARK

01 INTRO

41 ELYSION PARK

67 RESERVOIR

93 MORENO

129 NEUTRA

183 SCHINDLER

175 SUNSET JUNCTION

193 ATWATER

219 SILVER LAKE BLVD

239 SILVER LAKE ADJACENT

261 ACKNOWLEDGMENTS

WELCOME TO SILVERLAKE

SUNSET ★
JUNCTION

SINCE
1928

INTRODUCTION

Since the early twentieth century, this area has been populated by non-conformists…

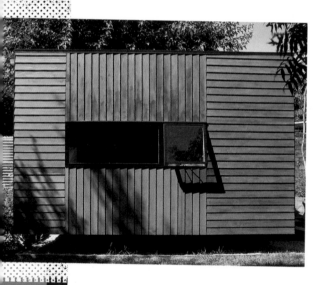

Silver Lake is one of those neighborhoods that has an amazing sense of its own style. I first moved here when I was starting graduate school at the Southern California Institute of Architecture, and it immediately seemed to me like the only place on earth that anyone—a budding architect especially—could ever want to live. I would take walks up in the hills past Frank Lloyd Wright's Ennis-Brown house, have drinks at Larry Nicola's restaurant designed by the then up-and-coming architecture office Morphosis (where I had a summer job), and hunt down houses by Rudolf Schindler (my favorite architect ever). Just a little ways east of Hollywood, the neighborhood spreads over hills and around a few lakes in an almost rustic way. Since the early twentieth century, this area has been populated by non-conformists, starting with its earliest settlers—the early silent movie studios and the actors (Charlie Chaplin! Tom Mix!), writers, and set painters that came with them. Later, in the 1930s and '40s, progressives, communists, artists, and a large Latino population all flocked to this enclave while the rest of the city grew more conservative and economically and racially divided. By the 1970s, Silver Lake had reinvented itself again as a gay neighborhood, a low-key counterpart to West Hollywood.

2

FAR LEFT
The Elliot Smith memorial wall on Sunset Boulevard.

LEFT
Lorcan O'Herlihy's Lexton McCarthy house.

One of the most visible results of this history is Silver Lake's wealth of modern residential architecture. The most famous local architects in the area, Rudolf Schindler and Richard Neutra, did some of their best experimental work here, but there are also fantastic houses by Craig Ellwood, John Lautner, Harwell Hamilton Harris, Gregory Ain, and Raphael Soriano. These architects, though of different generations, tend to share certain concerns: embracing new materials and colors, rethinking the uses and hierarchies of domestic spaces, and breaking down the barriers between indoors and out.

Today in Silver Lake there are several young firms, my own included, that aspire to continue in this tradition of low-key, experimental modernism. The new architects I put in this book are not doing mid-century historical revivalism, but trying out new ideas. Schindler really started the regional non-conformist modernism movement that I subscribe to. Silver Lake's architecture grew up parallel to international style modernism, but it developed without the formal orthodoxy. The bohemian strain was supported by three factors: the clients, the climate (all the sun, water, and swimming pools), and the vision of the architects themselves (many of them were European trained émigrés in the exalted company of Thomas Mann, Arnold Schoenberg, F.W. Murnau, and the like). This work is defined by informality, rawness, and a large dollop of hedonism.

The so-called bohemian modern lifestyle is illustrated here by the variety of people who live happily and comfortably in modern environments without sacrificing their individuality. The intent of this book is to capture a glimpse of the energy of the community.

OPPOSITE
Maximilian's Schell, an installation at Materials and Application by Ball-Nogues (Benjamin Ball and Gaston Nogues).

ABOVE
Blik Design graphics on Bestor Studio.

ECHO PARK

Echo Park is the neighborhood that sprawls through the hills alongside Silver Lake. There are a lot of simple, small wooden houses that were built at the turn of the last century as hunting shacks for downtown city dwellers.

A couple hangs out at Chango in the afternoon.

8

Though there isn't any hunting going on here these days, there are still some wild coyotes prowling around that live in the huge public park nearby. My first house ever was in Echo Park. Back in the 1980s, it was very cheap and had a gang problem (see local filmmaker Alison Anders' *Mi Vida Loca* for details), and I got a wreck of a little house through an ad in a newspaper. That was the first time I got to operate on a building as a "found object." My

9

then husband and I did things like cutting a big hole in the back wall facing the garden and filling it with a metal garage door that we could operate with a clicker from bed. It was the biggest dog door ever.

Echo Park has become a little more upscale lately, but it's managed to maintain its mellow, woodsy character. Jeb and Sandy Boardman, who live across the street from me, are leftist activists who have bought up many of the old shacks and rent them out, refusing to sell them because they want to preserve the character of the neighborhood. (Actually one of their houses has become the home of their pet pig Victoria, who has grown to be a rather large creature.) I built one of my first architectural projects here (Josh Oreck and Tina Carter's house, see page 20), and several of my colleagues have been doing new houses or experimental additions and remodels that are interesting but modest enough to hide on side streets or behind trees.

Background photograph of the lights above Dodger Staduim by Nancy Steiner.

LEFT
An exhibit of local artwork hangs at Chango Cafe.

The fashionable dogs of Echo Park, including Floyd *(opposite)* and Mike Diamond and Tamra Davis' dog, Rufus *(right)*.

The house I designed a few years ago for myself and my girls was a new beginning, of sorts.

I had left Los Angeles for the East Coast in 2001 to teach at Harvard University Graduate School of Design. I grew up in Cambridge, got my B.A. at Harvard, and spent summer vacations on the beach there, so it felt like home to me. My husband, two baby girls, and I moved into a big, rambling old house in Providence, Rhode Island, and I commuted back and forth. We chose Providence because we wanted to raise our daughters in a small city and be close to Block Island, where I had designed a small, minimalist but vernacular beach house in which we could spend our summers.

Only eight months later (just after September 11), I found myself packing again. Adam and I had decided to separate, and I moved back to Los Angeles, the place that I had come to realize was my home.

It was a difficult time for me and I needed a project. I wanted to design a home where I could raise my girls; a place that would be equally comfortable for children and grown-ups; and a refuge where we could all reclaim some equilibrium. I tried to envision this calm, loving environment as a three-dimensional structure. Childlike images of houses kept flashing through my mind.

One afternoon, when I was on my way home from a kooky new-age therapy session, I got lost in the Echo Park hills. Driving around, I came across a quarter-acre plot with a dilapidated cabin in the corner and a "For Sale" sign out in front. It had been a weekend cabin, built in the 1920s, which was moved from a nearby parcel to make way for a water tower. After standing abandoned for more than five years, all the neighbors assumed that the structure would be torn down to make way for condominiums or another McMansion.

I immediately decided that I had to have it. It looked just like the childlike drawing of a house that I had been picturing. It also sort of looked like the Unabomber cabin, which I had been thinking of as a strange new icon of

LEFT
A "before" shot of the cabin in Echo Park hills.

At night, the windows in the house glow.

11

barbara
BESTOR

ABOVE:
Beatrice and Charlotte play in the children's garden. The outdoor fire pit is the focal point of the outdoor living and dining area.

RIGHT:
A walkway connects the front garden area to the outdoor living space in the back.

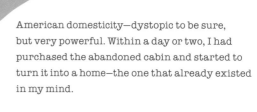

Our house through the eyes of Beatrice.

American domesticity—dystopic to be sure, but very powerful. Within a day or two, I had purchased the abandoned cabin and started to turn it into a home—the one that already existed in my mind.

I was subletting the Carter Oreck house a few blocks away and began to make daily visits to the new site with a construction crew headed by Monte Ross, a long time collaborator. The idea was first to strip the structure away to its bare bones, and then improvise. My budget for the renovation and landscaping was $250,000. I drafted no official plan. I just had drawings and ideas that I worked and reworked almost daily. I had never worked without formal plans on any projects for my regular clients before, so this was sort of freeing. Maybe a little scary too, but certainly exhilarating.

I built around a few key pieces of furniture and built-ins, starting with a nineteenth century Steinway upright piano I had bought back in Providence. It became the centerpiece of the living room wall, with a custom sized window above it to frame it and a pair of oversized floating bookcases on each side.

In the kitchen, I designed a huge, five-by-ten-foot island that anchors the room but also defines zones of activity without visual obstruction. For windows, I made one long vertical cut on the front elevation (all glass now) and another long horizontal cut on the back.

In the open first-floor room, I used paint color to divide the space: the living room is a deep magenta and the kitchen is a vibrant red. To create completely indestructible countertops, I installed a laboratory material called TopLab. The cabinets are made of MDF, a recycled wood pulp that costs about half as much as most wood cabinet materials, and they are finished with six coats of lacquer for durability. The result is a warm honey color.

The stark, white hallway, an irresistible surface for markers, has been painted with high-gloss paint (easy to wipe) on the lower portion and a flat paint on the upper, giving the illusion of two shades.

I like reading in the morning at the dining room table.

A wooden staircase, painted hot yellow, leads upstairs to the yellow, pink, and plywood attic bedroom the girls share. Marimekko curtains, a classic 1966 print called Unikko, are suspended on a tracking system inspired by hospital room curtains. Even if it's just visual privacy, it works. At night the girls draw their curtains and it really cuts down on the chatter.

My own downstairs bedroom is a tiny 120 square feet. I installed the same sliding drapery system with a cheap quilted liner fabric, which I cut with scissors and left unfinished. My study across the hall is lined with custom-colored wallpaper by my friend, the graphic artist Geoff McFetridge.

The overall organization of the house is very simple, but multiple paths through the house are possible so that grownups at cocktail parties and children at birthday parties can circulate in endless loops.

Most days, the two girls play games that have them circulating freely between indoors and out, just like I had hoped they would. They can ride their bikes from the front yard through the house and out to the back without much effort. They get to experience in their daily life the modernist dream of indoor-outdoor living. I'm raising real California girls!

The front door is storefront one-way mirror glass.

Geoff McFetridge designed the wallpaper in the office.

I collaborated with the terrific garden designer Stephanie Bartron to create playful, colorful outdoor areas that offset the house's dark exterior. In the deep front yard there is a sandbox, a hammock, and a pair of plastic McDonald's benches that I bought at a yard sale for six bucks apiece. The vegetable garden, specifically planned for children, contains Icelandic poppies, pansies, lettuces, and Swiss chard. Nearby is a fish- and plant-filled fountain that greets visitors as they walk through the courtyard entrance, which is surrounded by vine-filled trellises. When I was discussing the design and plantings with Stephanie, we agreed that the overall feel we wanted was "industrial romantic." There are simple, raw materials (poured concrete, fencing made from steel reinforcing mesh, rough redwood planks) counterbalanced by lush, violet-tinged plants and flowers. Throughout the summer, incredible, brightly colored dragonflies buzz around different areas of the garden.

The outdoor living area is an extension of the indoors.

We also designed a poured-concrete seating area and fire pit for the back patio. We eat many of our meals at the outdoor table, which is made from square tube steel and a durable, inexpensive wood decking material called Ironwood. I eventually want to put a ladder up the side of the palm tree and create a treehouse.

The house is sided with a sustainable fiber cement board called Hardiplank, which, along with ordinary stucco, is one of the cheapest siding materials available. I installed commercial aluminum storefront windows and doors, saving money over conventional residential windows. The exterior is painted with a mixture of black and blue that looks dark during the day but softer and bluer as the sun goes down. One neighbor kept coming by and asking if that was really the color I planned to keep the house. I think they thought it was going to look like a big Goth Lolita playhouse!

After bedtime, the dark blue siding of the house disappears in the darkness, the windows glow, and the moon reflects and sparkles off the metal roof. That's my favorite time at the house. It is a simple house, and a happy one.

LEFT
My house on Block Island was the inspiration for Echo Park. My friend K.C. Perry snapped a shot of it.

FAR LEFT
The stairs that lead to the girls room.

ABOVE LEFT
Marimekko hangs in the bathroom.

ABOVE
Me and the girls in the garden hammock. The fire pit glows regularly.

TINA CARTER + JOSH ORECK

Just after I completed the Haurum Collings house in Mount Washington, my first new house for a pair of artists, Tina Carter and Josh Oreck gave me a great commission in Echo Park. They are both artists—a painter and a filmmaker— who wanted a house that was creative and open, and would allow a collaborative relationship with their architect. They bought a piece of land right on the edge of a huge public park in Echo Park and imagined a live/work home with the potential for gallery space and lots of entertaining. The house we made, which is nicknamed the "show house," is based on the most common, low-tech building system—two-by- four framing and insulation, which in Los Angeles is called "Type 5" construction. We liked the idea of letting the banality of construction be on display here and there.

FAR LEFT
Daytime view of
the Carter Oreck
house.

The inside of
the house is on
display at night.

The site is a woodsy hillside with a couple of views that we wanted to frame. We actually created views to the interior guts of the house as well as the vistas around it, all of which are showcased using an extruded storefront window system that sits just outside the exterior walls: At the back of the house, there is a view through all three levels, with a single continuous window unit that shows floor framing, insulation, windows, and concrete foundations in one long take. The interior is arranged around a three-story bookcase/staircase tower made of medium density fiberboard, and the bearing walls of the house were left in their original plywood.

All of the wood interiors and the foliage outside the windows give the spaces a very light, tree house–like feeling. The lowest floor, however, has walls of poured and sanded concrete that make it cavelike and an excellent place to hang out in the summer. Since the house was built, the family has expanded, and we are now planning an addition, for which we might use mirror glass cladding to reflect the surrounding forest.

LEFT
An extruded storefront window system sits just outside the exterior walls.

RIGHT
The bookcase runs through all three floors.

23

The house was built with views of the surrounding landscape as well as the interior guts of the house.

25

NORMAN MILLAR

Norman Millar is a fantastic architect who is my mentor and was, for a time, my partner (we did a neat modernist craftsman house in the Pacific Palisades for Pat and Maiya Verrone). Nowadays, he is the chair of the architecture department at Woodbury University, and we live just up the street from each other in the hills of Echo Park.

Norman often sleeps outside in his Zen den, a structure he designed and built himself in his backyard. A contractor gave him some redwood boards and some multipaned windows left over from a job, and he decided to challenge himself and see if he could build a structure alone. "I wanted to see what one person could do, one nail at a time," he says. The ten-by-ten-by-sixteen structure is where he reads the paper, sleeps, and soaks in the custom tub that he installed. "It is a very peaceful place," he says.

When he bought the lot in 1989, the only thing on it was a tiny shack that was built back in 1904. It was a cute little white house with redwood siding but no foundation. The plan was to fix it up enough to live there temporarily, and then eventually replace it. There was a large front yard with little grass and no driveway. "I wanted a driveway, so that was the first thing I decided to take care of," he recalls. "I picked up a shovel and got to work." The driveway project took about a year to complete.

Lush tropical vegetation closes in on the entrance to Norman's house. The gate was designed by metal artist Gale McCall.

Norman spends most of his time outdoors in the gardens he planted.

My friend, metal artist Gale McCall, designed a front entry gate that has the pattern of a man biting a dog. It was during the installation of that gate that Norman learned how to weld. It was also around that time that he became obsessed with plants and set out to create a lush tropical environment on his property. I remember him taking special trips around town when the gardeners were out, picking up unusual cuttings of plants to add to the collection. He has desert plants next to tropical plants, and they coexist nicely with the help of a drip irrigation system. "I have over ten euphorias, which you propagate by simply cutting," he says, surveying his garden. "I really never envisioned that the trees would take off like they have."

From March through Thanksgiving, Norman spends most of his time outdoors, and the meandering paths and patio create spaces to entertain friends and family. He is currently planning an addition that will cause the Zen den to have to come down. "It served its purpose for the time, and now there will be something different in its place," says Norman. "I like the idea of working on something new."

29

30

CAITLIN WYLDE

Caitlin Wylde, a painter and sculptor, found her dream house on the bulletin board of the Back Door Bakery on Silver Lake Boulevard. The Tudor-style house was for sale by the owners, and she instantly fell in love with it. "I call it my wacky little castle," she smiles. "And it's an amazing place to get work done."

The house sits on the edge of Elysian Park, where she often goes for inspiration, or to walk her four dogs: Sam, Cleo, Angus, and Dodger. Originally from South Dartmouth, Massachusetts, she left to attend the San Francisco Art Institute and eventually landed in Los Angeles to pursue her art. In the sunnier section of the house, her studio houses large-scale sculptural objects and dioramas, which will eventually go into a show.

LEFT

Caitlin Wylde's dogs often hang out in her studio.

Large scale sculptural objects and dioramas will eventually all be part of a show.

31

The inspiration for her art comes from her family history on the East Coast. "I was poking around old family trees and researching my family history," she says. "Now, white colonial men, sperm whales, bears, trees, and forests have all become focal points in my work."

She recently created a series of silhouettes of Puritan men doing impure things, and her dioramas of forests and unchartered territory seem to directly tie in with the early Americana theme. One of her current projects, a polar bear, is a play on scale and stands at well over seven feet tall.

The interior of the "wacky little castle" shows her eclectic cozy style.

C.O.A.

In 1999 the three architects of the Central Office of Architecture (COA) were approached by a couple who had a very specific commission request but had yet to purchase a property. The couple, a philosophy professor and an art director for film, had lived in a loft downtown and wanted to recreate the open floor plan, high ceilings, and spaciousness that it offered.

Russell N. Thomsen, one of the three partners at the firm, remembers making a sketch of the new building before they designed it. "I envisioned it like a luminous box," he says. They inverted the typical order of a house and designed it so that the lower ground level is a series of small bedrooms and the upstairs is an open living space. "When you go up the hill and enter the house, you are confronted with the building. When you go up the stairs and reach the second level, you are hit with the captivating view from all sides," he describes.

They envisioned the house as a luminous box in the evening, fully glowing.

Translucent panels span the east side to create privacy, and the clear storefront glazing along the west side is protected from the harsh sunlight by a full height steel shade structure. I like how the project incorporates the international style sensibility of the 1920s with low cost materials that are very contemporary.

FACING PAGE
Transluscent panels
span the east side to
create privacy.

The entrance on the
ground level leads to all
the bedrooms.

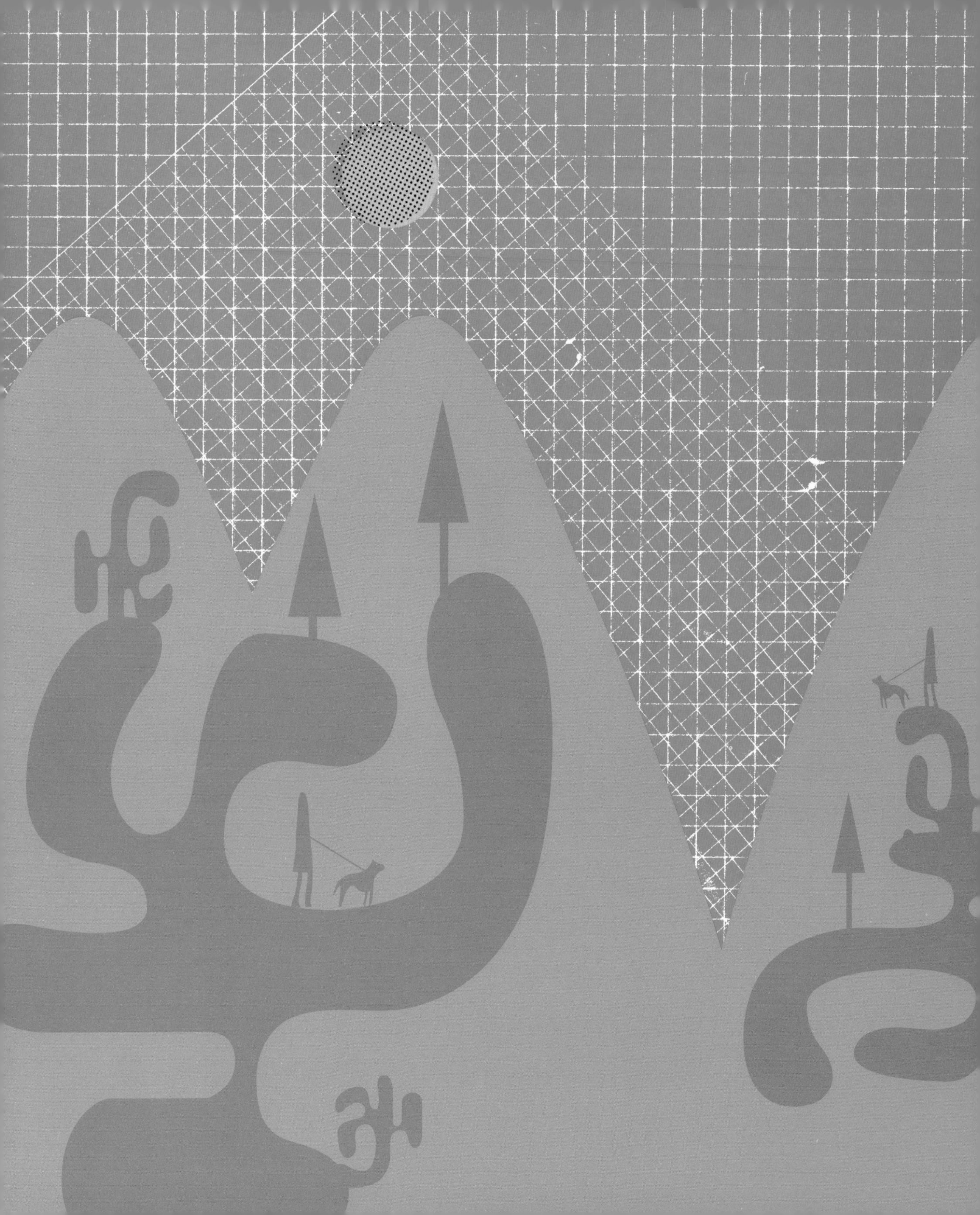

ELYSIAN PARK

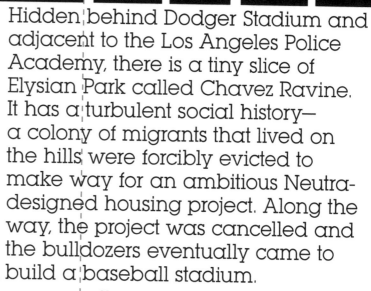

Hidden behind Dodger Stadium and adjacent to the Los Angeles Police Academy, there is a tiny slice of Elysian Park called Chavez Ravine. It has a turbulent social history— a colony of migrants that lived on the hills were forcibly evicted to make way for an ambitious Neutra-designed housing project. Along the way, the project was cancelled and the bulldozers eventually came to build a baseball stadium.

Now the community has its own church, school, and town hall, and many of the locals have resided there for generations. The neighborhood is basically in the middle of a public park and is cut off from the adjacent Chinatown by the elderly 110 freeway. It is in this little pocket, officially known as Elysian Heights, that my friends Roger and Eika, Judy and Erik, and Jon Huck all live on the same block, connected by little paths and a sense of community in the wilderness.

There is a special hidden path that leads from Judy Kameon and Erik Otsea's garden to Jon Huck's house. "We decided it was crazy to take the road all the time. I thought, he might as well have his own path, so I made him one," says Judy, a well-known garden designer and the owner of Elysian Landscapes.

I have known Judy since the late '80s when she opened a very influential neighborhood art gallery and boutique called "Livestock." These days, I often see her at dinner at her house where she hosts a regular "special friends" night with Jon. He buys the food and brings a special guest, and Judy and Erik prepare an amazing meal in their colorful, old-fashioned kitchen.

Judy studied painting in school, and that was what she was doing when she moved into her small cottage. "No one wanted to live here back then," she says, "but it was affordable and I had a great Dane puppy and a big fenced yard." Slowly, she added a second lot to the property and built a studio. That giant lot began to lure her away from her painting, and she started spending most of her days creating a garden. "I looked at gardening in the same way I viewed painting, as a creative practice," she says.

Once she had finished making a series of outdoor spaces at home, she decided to open a restaurant and serve food in the garden. On the opening night, friends approached her to design their gardens. That was the beginning of Elysian Landscapes (and the end of the restaurant!). Today it is very clear when you're driving around Silver Lake which gardens were designed by Judy. She has a true appreciation for architecture and her designs always compliment the structures they surround.

JUDY KAMEON

42

Connie Butler and Dave Schafer's Schindler house (see chapter on Schindler) is a prime example. "It is about the people who live in the house, the house itself, the site, and hopefully a lot more than that when it's completed," says Judy. She designed a palette that worked with the warm gray-green tones that define most Schindler houses. Several types of ornamental grasses terracing down the steep hillside evoke the feeling of a meadow, and plants with a very graphic color palette—pampas grass, trailing rosemary, and bronze phormium—line the stairway to the street. Like the built-ins that most Schindler houses include, stairs also act as benches and create seating at the top of the garden.

Today, Judy and her team of designers have branched out into commercial garden design. They recently designed the twelve-acre garden at the new Parker Hotel in Palm Springs, and the park and courtyard of the new Marc Jacobs stores in West Hollywood. Judy and her husband Erik also design a line of outdoor furniture called Plain Air. The line consists of '50s and '60s inspired chairs, tables, and day beds fabricated from powder-coated stainless steel. "There is nothing I love more than hanging outside here on the day bed in my garden," says Judy, "It gives me time to think about things, read the paper, and nap."

A dining terrace overlooks the pool.

RIGHT
Inside, Judy collects vintage pottery and cooks on a bright red vintage stove.

FAR LEFT
A friend of Judy's plays in the fountain.

LEFT
Dinner parties are a regular occurrence at the Kameon residence.

Judy has been working with a company called Tri Star while designing the thirteen-acre garden at the new Parker Palm Springs Hotel. Because they planted so many citrus trees on the property, this cocktail was named after them.

TRI STAR COCKTAIL

Squeeze a whole lemon—preferably just picked off the tree—into a cocktail glass.

Add:

Crushed ice to fill glass

½ shot homemade grapefruit bar syrup

(see below)

1 shot of vodka

splash of sparkling soda

candied kumquat for garnish

TO MAKE GRAPEFRUIT BAR SYRUP:
Boil 2 cups water with 2 cups sugar and add the rind of a whole grapefruit. Strain and store in a glass jar.

47

ABOVE
A new addition creates space for her office and studio.

Roger Herman

Roger Herman is a painter and a professor in the art department at UCLA. He and his wife Eika Aoshima, a photographer and clothing manufacturer, live in a pair of houses that were designed by Fred Fisher. The first house and studio is one of my favorite houses in Los Angeles.

When I first met Roger in the late '80s (at Gorky's in downtown Los Angeles), he boasted about how he and his then wife, Tamra Davis, were building a giant plywood box to live in. And he was quite accurate. The house's deceptively simple form is made from rough materials, including plywood floors and walls. "Over the years, the plywood has become worn and has turned almost a honey color, which I love," he beams. The spaces within the giant box are grand and surprising in their complexity: interlocking rooms at multiple levels, and internal windows that allow you a peek at the new work in the studio as you pass through a corridor. Roger's woodcuts and paintings hang all over the house and studio, bringing color and scale to the large rooms. In his office there is a wall of art, which he has collected over years of teaching. His collection is vast and eclectic ranging from Raymond Pettibone to Nick Lowe.

Roger's painting studio. A corner of his living space shows a painting and his pottery.

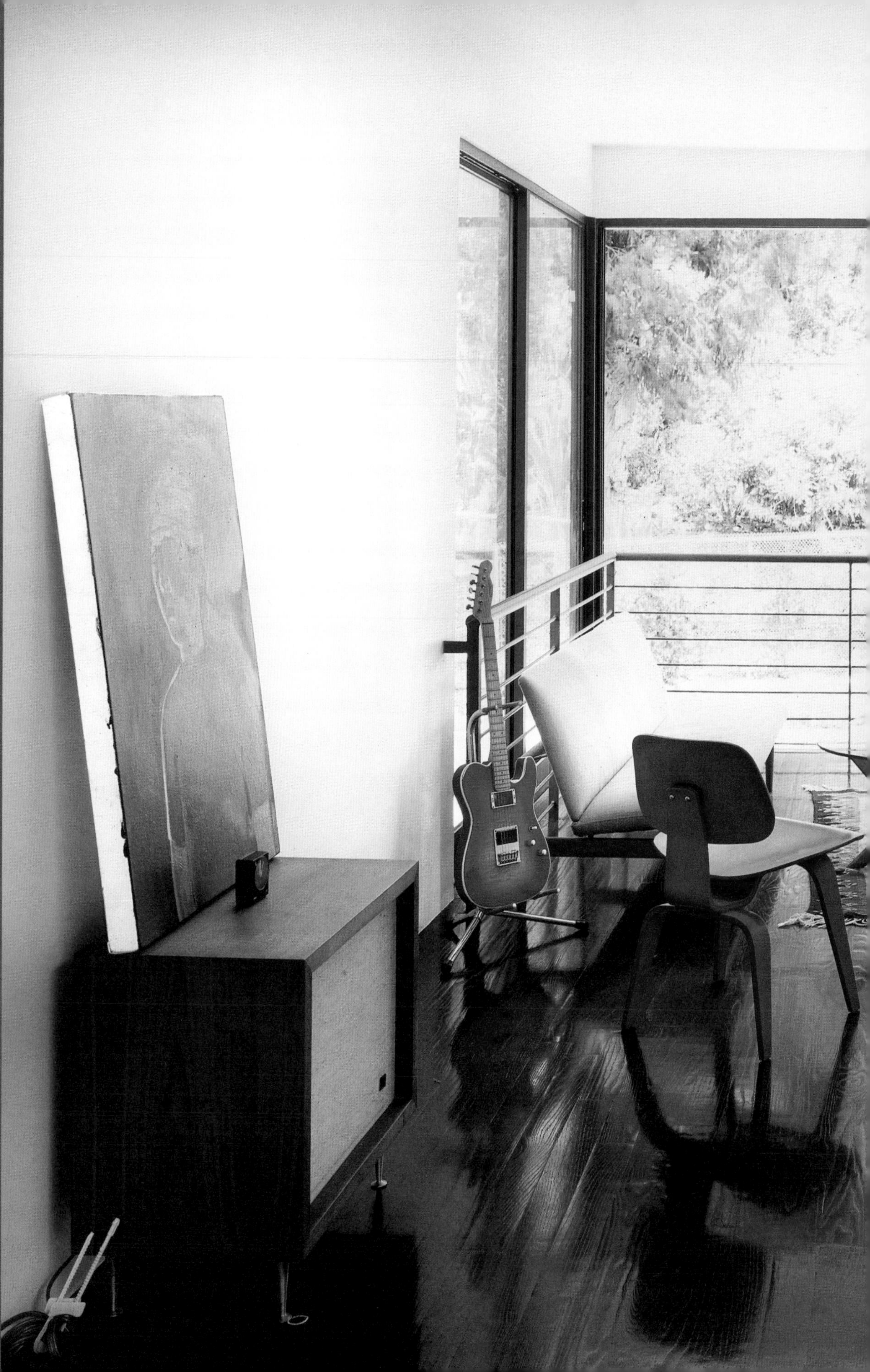

Eikas designs hang on a
wardrobe rack.

The whole house is well set up for entertaining. A table that seats at least twelve runs along one side of the living room, and there is a huge covered porch just off the kitchen that holds another overscale table. Their dogs, which run freely inside and out, include a giant German shepherd named Huck, after neighbor Jon Huck.

The most recent addition to the compound is a tall, narrow metal building, also designed by Fred Fisher, which is Eika's hideaway. "This is where I work on my clothing line which is called Twig. I work on my photography and I watch Japanese videos," she says. "This is my space where I can do whatever I want."

BELOW
Roger's personal art collection.

RIGHT
The exterior of the property. Far Right: An outdoor dining area. Below Right: The new space next to the old— with the pool.

"The nice thing about living here is that I'm tucked away from all the commotion of the city. It is very peaceful here and I know all my neighbors, so if I want to have a conversation or take a break from work, I don't have to go far."

55

Back in the main house, there is a room dedicated to
Roger's new passion—glazed ceramic vessels. "I decided
that I wanted to learn this technique, so I worked with
a well-known potter named Lisa Yu to learn," he says.
The imperfect pots and vases are erotic images of
animals, people, and objects.

"The nice thing about living here is that I'm tucked
away from all the commotion of the city. It is very
peaceful here and I know all my neighbors, so if I want
to have a conversation or take a break from work, I
don't have to go far."

Raw plywood floors run throughout
the house.

Piles of Roger's pottery are displayed on occasional tables in one section of the house.

JON HUCK

It was Judy Kameon who showed Jon Huck, a composer, music supervisor, and photographer, the lot next door to her in Elysian Park. "I wanted to build something for myself that was more like a workspace than a conventional house," Huck says.

The house that Jon built is a simple, modern structure with two tall stories and mostly open space. There is a private music studio, and upstairs are two enclosed bedrooms, but that's about it. The public spaces are all open, including the sparsely decorated double-height living room. A long couch sits along one wall, instruments are scattered haphazardly, and an enormous collection of music and books give the place the feel of a library. A well-worn piano sits in one corner.

Jon works constantly and does all of his work at home. But he is also the consummate gentleman about town, and at one point he was posting daily updates to a website of his party pictures from out and about. I like to have lunch with Jon at least once a week, but often I have to fight to keep my place in line. He also has a very regular output of excellent private label mixed CDs that always come with good titles and found-art covers. Recently he had a show of his portraits of friends, called simply "Breakfast." It included just over a hundred portraits of people with their everyday breakfast that he shot around the neighborhood over a six-month period. Jon also shot the portraits for this book, bringing to them the warmth and eye for human detail his photographs always manifest.

LEFT
Jon's work area and piano.

Jon Huck's living area.

62

An excerpt from "Breakfast."

The kitchen is tucked under the staircase.

63

RVOIR

In the 1990s, my then husband and I moved into a 1906 Craftsman house on a cul-de-sac with an absolutely fantastic view of the Silver Lake Reservoir. Every time I came home, it felt as if I had left a Los Angeles street and opened my back door to a bucolic vista in northern Vermont, placid lake and all.

We furnished the place in a decidedly *un*Craftsman-like style, with a hodge podge of modern furniture, thrift store finds, and a stuffed and mounted trout—okay, maybe it was a *little* Craftsman. We painted most of the rooms in very rich, saturated colors: burgundy ("B-boy burgundy" we called it), deep blue, forest green.

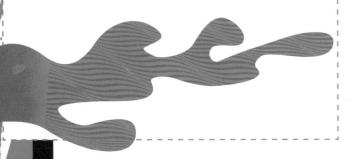

We sold the house to its current caretakers, filmmaker Dante Ariola and Suzanne Rynne, when my family and I moved to the East Coast. When I got back to Los Angeles and started a practice again, they wanted to do some additions (I had done a master bedroom wing before moving), so we expanded the kitchen and basement guest room, and Stephanie Bartron planned out a new garden. I still love this house— the traditional architectural details are simultaneously elegant and rough. And we continue to work on it, adding more outdoor rooms and a swimming pool that will float just above the reservoir view.

A view of the reservoir.

We furnished the place in a decidedly *un*-Craftsman-like style, with a hodge podge of modern furniture, thrift store finds, and a stuffed and mounted trout—okay, maybe it was a *little* Craftsman.

The craftsman house was furnished with an eclectic mix of styles—both modern and traditional.

A new kitchen was
added recently.

DYLAN ROBERTSON

"Spending time in this room is like being outdoors," says Emily Jagoda of Hedge Design Collective. She assisted in the design and renovation of the tract house, a duplex that was built in 1965.

The downstairs apartment where Dylan Robertson and his girlfriend Katie live is about 800 square feet. There is a small workspace, kitchen and bedroom, which is part of the main house.

Dylan and Emily got rid of the ugly tract house elements, like green shag carpet, and replaced them with top notch mid-century materials, like cork. Emily used an inexpensive fiberglass material called Ornite to create the large-paned walls. "It has an opalescent quality, which creates privacy when it is completely shut," she explains.

72

LEFT
A path leads to Dylan's house.

Emily Jagoda designed the addition, which the owners say makes them feel like they live outdoors.

74

French doors lead to the living space, which is essentially like being outside. When the giant Ornite doors are open, you are outdoors. "Dylan tells me they love it when it rains because it doesn't leak, yet they feel like they are in the midst of it," says Emily.

"Spending time in this room is like being outdoors," says Emily Jagoda of Hedge Design Collective.

FAR LEFT
The upper deck protrudes over the indoor-outdoor living space.

LEFT
The indoor-outdoor living space.

ABOVE
Ornite, the material used like glass, is translucent and shimmers both in the evening light and daytime.

An outdoor dining area doubles as a party space and outdoor movie theater.

SARAH CAPLAN

Sarah Caplan lives in a house that is almost a perfect square. It is hidden away on a quiet street but exudes its modern influence on the hillside below. "I liked the idea that you could put the house together from Home Depot," says Sarah.

The house took a year to build and was completed in 2001. British friends designed it overseas, so it was important that there were no variances on the building permit. "It was literally straight to code when we started building, and there was nothing very fancy, nothing custom," she says. "There is also a very low level of finish, which kept the cost down."

The downstairs floor is all foundation walls and concrete floors. The chimney, which comes up through the middle of the living room, is an aluminum chimney liner. The windows are large aluminum frames placed at a height that makes curtains unnecessary. "It's a fairly small house, but the open plan gives it the illusion of space" says Sarah, who lives there with her teenage daughter Stella. The upstairs floor is just the right size for Sarah's frequent dinner parties for ten or so, where guests move through kitchen,

dining, and living areas, circulating around the central stair and dodging a very intimidating high-tech cello.

The exterior garden design is a combination of geometric forms and vibrant colors and Sarah is still on the hunt for bright red plants to accentuate that scheme. She and Pia Dominguez, a landscape designer, created a terrace garden with a variety of grasses. There is a round slab of cement on one terrace level that serves as the platform for a dining table and chairs. Steps that were designed to be part of the terrace double as auditorium seating when she projects movies out in the garden. "I love to sit outside in the afternoon sun or in the evening when the garden is all lit up," she says.

"I'm really content."

77

ABOVE
The interior living area connects with the kitchen.

ABOVE LEFT
A series of terraces in the back are planted with an interesting mix of grasses.

RAQUEL MUNOZ-FLORES

Raquel Munoz-Flores remembers the day she and her boyfriend happened upon the Raphael Soriano house for sale. Tucked in off the street, it wasn't much to look at from the outside, but the moment she walked in, she knew she had to have it. Although she wasn't looking for an architecturally significant house at the time, when she saw the Soriano house, she realized that underneath all the years of updating and renovating, there was a sound house with great bones and a strong history.

Soriano, one of the great California Case Study architects, designed and built the house in 1939 for the Meyers family. Soriano was known for his innovative use of steel and aluminum and his keen interest in prefabricated modular construction at a low cost. Just after it was built, the Meyers' house was featured in a design magazine article about homes that cost under $5,000.

The house stayed in the family and the Meyers' son raised his three daughters there. It was a family that appreciated music and the arts. There was a row of metal filing cabinets designed to hold sheet music, and secret cabinets and built-ins for storing musical instruments. "I heard that everyone knew the Meyers' family," Raquel says. "The three daughters were all musically inclined and they had legendary New Year's parties where an orchestra would play in the backyard and the whole family would jam. They were the type of family that always had a student living with them; the type of house where there was always something interesting going on."

When Raquel purchased the house from the Meyers' daughters, they had just lost their parents in a tragic car accident. She knew it was difficult for them to give it up and she felt an immense responsibility. One afternoon when she was in the midst of redoing it, one of the daughters stopped by with her family to show them the house that she grew up in. "I was so nervous that she wouldn't like it, but when she walked in she gasped and was genuinely pleased. I think the house probably looked a lot like it did when she was a child," Raquel says, "before all the additions and the carpeting."

When Raquel moved in, the house was in need of work. Slowly, she started to take it back to its roots. The '70s carpet was scrapped but the original built-in sofa was restored and reupholstered. A neighbor's vintage steel kitchen cabinetry, which had been a prize on "The Price Is Right," was salvaged, refurbished and installed in the galley-style kitchen. Many of the pieces of furniture in the house are in keeping with the era, and the shelves and

Raquel refurbished the vintage steel kitchen.

79

Pieces from Raquel's collection of art are displayed throughout the living areas.

TOP RIGHT
From the outside, the house seems much smaller than it is.

walls are lined with pieces of art that she has collected locally. There is a small group of prints by David Weidman, a prominent artist who worked in advertising and animation in the '50s and '60s, that she picked up at a flea market. A portrait of Robert Wagner's mother was found at a thrift store. There is a large painting by Mark Gonzalez, a local skater artist, and a small nude by another prominent skater artist, Ed Templeton. The large concrete and steel table in the garden was built and designed by artist friend Donnie Molls. And David McCaully, a friend and interior designer, designed the chairs and coffee table in the living room.

When Raquel was cleaning out the house, she came across two rusty cots on a deck. One of the neighbors told her that the Meyers often liked to sleep outside under the stars. "There is a lot of romance in this house," Raquel remarks, "I'd like to some day raise my family here and live in the house the way the Meyers did."

The Meyers' Daughters Reflect

SHARON MEYERS

"I remember the Ping-Pong table outside being the center of all our activities. We had all the birthday parties on it and all the holiday dinners. There was no formal dining room in the house so the Ping-Pong porch was where we usually gathered. I think we were probably poor but we had no sense of that. I never remember feeling like I ever needed anything. And I remember being very happy that way."

"Our parents were famous for taking people in and, in essence, adopting them. Over the years, we had close to twenty different people staying with us, some for short stays, others for longer periods of time. It was interesting because when my parents died, all of those people came to the memorial service and stayed in the house. They were truly like family members."

JUDY GREENE

"Space was certainly different back then. We eventually added the addition which gave us another bedroom, but the close confines of the house never bothered us. I remember the living room—it truly was a living room. Everything happened in that room. We did our homework there. We practiced our music there."

"I remember we were very different than most families on our block—we were Jewish Democrats who read books and played music. None of the other houses in the neighborhood had books. Our parents loved to teach and share any sort of knowledge they had. We had a large blackboard, and I have vivid memories of gathering around it and listening to my father try to explain things to us."

TERRY MEYERS

"We purchased the property from Grandma and Grandpa Meyers in 1948 for $10,000. Before, we were cramped up in a one-bedroom apartment somewhere else in Silver Lake and we desperately needed more space. Our parents used to tell us stories about how when the house was built, it was so modern and different that all the neighbors were freaking out."

"They had the large master bedroom and we shared the other one which had bunks. Because they both played—my mom played cello and my dad played the violin—we grew up with music. Other musicians often came over to play, too, and there were few nights when we went to sleep without listening to music. Our parents were famous for throwing an all night music marathon on New Year's, when they would play music for twenty-four hours straight. All their friends from various string quartets and orchestras would come and play."

The outdoor garden area directly off the living area. This is where the famous Ping-Pong table doubled as family dinner table and tournament board.

When a house on Cove Avenue, which was formerly owned by Edward (Tink) Adams, the founder of the Art Center College of Design, came on the market, the owner was adamant about selling it to an Art Center graduate. The 1951 house had not been steadily occupied for many years and had been used mainly for Art Center events.

When Glenn Lawson and Grant Fenning heard that the house was for sale, they jumped at the opportunity. They met as students in the environmental design program at the Art Center College of Design and felt a strong tie to the school and its founder. "I think it's nice for the people who live here to really appreciate the history of the house and the school," says Glenn.

When they purchased the house, the first order of business was reviving the orange details. Tink Adams had a fondness for orange and he thought that the liberal use of orange dots was a good way to add a splash of color to Art Center materials. The dots are part of the graphic identity of the school today. Glenn and Grant found original cans of orange paint in the garage that dated back to the fifties or sixties, and had it matched. All the entry doors in the house and garage are painted in original Art Center orange.

In 1967, James Delong, an architect who studied with Frank Lloyd Wright, designed an addition and did a major renovation of the house. The only part of the original house that remains is the kitchen. Glenn and Grant left the original kitchen intact and added a few black-and-white wedding photographs of Tink and his wife, Virginia, which were taken at the house in 1951. Changes to the rest of the house have been

GLENN LAWSON

relatively minor. They opened up a few rooms to better utilize the space and laid commercial grade sea grass matting in part of the house.

The house sits on a hill and the landscape is built on a series of terraces with paths. Landscape designer and grass specialist John Greenley planted an eclectic mix of grass varieties from around the world. Glenn and Grant spend most of their time outside and often have friends over.

Most of the rooms have spectacular views and there are patios on both sides of the house. "We basically follow the light," Glenn says. In the bedroom there are Japanese paper and wood sliders, which allow the light to come in but still create privacy. "In the sixties they really japonified everything," he explains. Their collection of vividly colored Japanese bud vases and sake containers fits right in.

The Japanese influenced living room includes furniture designed by Grant and Glenn.

ABOVE LEFT
A vintage sake vessel collection.

ABOVE RIGHT
A large bookcase houses a collection of pottery and ceramics.

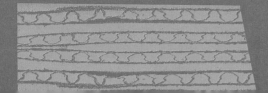

grant fenning

The gardens outside the house are connected by a winding path.

Most of the rooms have spectacular views and there are patios on both sides of the house. "We basically follow the light," Glenn says.

Glenn and Grant have decorated the rest of
house with period furniture and pieces from
their own furniture collection which made
its debut in New York in 2002. They have a
small showroom for the furniture on Beverly
Boulevard and they also own a store in
Pasadena called Room 107, which showcases
their furniture and a variety of period pieces.

88

Old black and white photographs of Tink Adams at his second wedding were found in a back closet when Glenn and Grant purchased the house.

A letter from Mardy Adams, Tink's daughter

When a house was first built on this site there were no city streets, no city stairs, no other houses, and no lake. We were later told that a civil engineer who planned future land use for the city of Los Angeles had deemed these two lots "the best" and acquired them for himself. He and a son built a simple, rustic two-room cottage of redwood, and they started planting trees. Lots of trees. When we bought the property in 1942 it was so overgrown that the house could not be seen from the street—or anywhere else.

My father had been reading want ads for months, knowing that such a find existed somewhere and that its condition would not appeal to most people. The more hopeless it might appear to others, the more he could do—if it were in the right location. This was World War II and people weren't buying real estate. When the house finally did appear in a want ad, my father was determined to finance it somehow. A scruffy little handmade house in a jungle of overgrowth—perfect. With a loan from my grandmother it was possible for us to buy it at just about $5,000. The lake could not be seen from the house. In fact there were no windows that opened. The first thing that was done was the removal of twenty-five palm trees. And this was a tricky matter as no truck could be brought onto the property. It became a question of whether the truck pulled a tree up or a tree pulled the truck down. Somehow, with a lot of anxious yelling, the job was accomplished. And we could see the lake!

My father found a wonderful old carpenter named Mr. Potts, and together they worked out the least expensive ways to open up the house, using as much of the original structure as possible. It then had two bedrooms, one bath, an L-shaped kitchen and a central dressing room. It also had a wonderful fireplace. Between the house and the retaining wall on the east side was a narrow walkway that got very muddy when it rained. Eventually it was cemented in, making it easier to get wood for our fireplace, for one thing.

What this did, however, was block moisture into the underpinnings of the house. One day we came home to find the stove had fallen through the floor. There never has been a solid foundation; the original house was probably sitting on a few bricks. At the same time the house was getting attention, the garden was getting a new life—and a very different look. My father, who grew up in southern Arizona, developed a love of trees and read endlessly about them. Combining this feeling for trees with his deep appreciation of oriental art resulted in a garden of rare beauty and tranquility. There's a special quality to a mature garden. I think of it as contentment. One very special tree, which is a visual focal point of the living room, is a marvelous old pine which was born and raised in Japan as a giant bonsai. It came to the U.S. in a box with a sister tree for an exposition in 1915. This was in San Diego, I believe. They may well have been gifts from the Japanese government. In any case, they fell into terrible neglect when the Japanese nurserymen, along with so many other Japanese Americans, were incarcerated during World War II. My father found this abandoned prize in the back of a nursery he was visiting after the war, and he quickly recognized its true quality. Getting it home and into the ground was another matter. I don't remember what year Howard Hughes's "spruce goose" was moved through the L.A. city streets (at night), but my dad went to the same people, Star House Movers, to get them to move this heavy, cumbersome giant in a box. A big hole had been prepared at the edge of the deck, but lowering the tree into its box and not disturbing its meager sail took much patience and skill—and a lot of sweating and holding of breaths. I couldn't watch.

The present house, which is really the third version, was designed by Albert A. Cooling and built in the '60s. The exception is the later addition of a cantilevered section which was designed by James De Long. This is composed of a large bedroom, glass on three sides, and an adjoining bath, all surrounded by a deck, rather like an exotic and palatial tree house. For many people who visited over the years it became much more than a wonderful house in a peaceful garden—it became a true oasis, a time out from the rest of the busy world. It is a place to nurture one's spirit and to remember the calm of the center.

MORENO

The fanciest bit of Silver Lake is the hill where Moreno Drive and Micheltorena Street run along the reservoir.

The neighborhood was built up between the 1930s and 1960s and now includes several modern landmarks. These days, the hills are overrun by young families with children. If you drive down any street, you'll have to slow down to about two miles per hour so as not to interfere with the strollers, joggers, and dog walkers that are out and about at all hours.

Further down the street on Micheltorena is a heavily remodeled and transformed '40s house that has captured the neighborhood's interest with its innovative self-expression. Almost daily the owners change their running LED message that always includes the house numbers with some additional commentary. It might be a quote from situationist Guy Debord or a welcome to the children arriving for a playdate that day. The house is the brainchild of architect Joe Day and his wife Nina Hachigian. Their house represents the new Silver Lake domesticity: family-friendly while progessive socially and aesthetically.

Spanning seven lots up the road on Micheltorena is John Lautner's "Silvertop," one of the architectural highlights of Silver Lake. Perched high on the hill, its arcing concrete roof can be seen from vantage points all around the neighborhood. It even has a cantilevered tennis court that is probably the coolest place to play tennis in Los Angeles. (One architect friend of mine has a friend with

LED display at the entrance to Joe Day's house.

a key to the court, and we constantly discuss how we might get permission and a key of our own!) It was built in 1957 by Keith Reiner and finished by the current owners, the Burchills, who raised their children in this expressionistic modern palace. When we went to photograph it, the Burchills invited my daughter Beatrice to swim in the infinity pool that looks over the reservoir, making her possibly the luckiest swimmer in town.

John Lautner came to southern California in the late '30s to supervise the construction of Frank Lloyd Wright's Sturges house. When it was finished, he decided to start his own practice. His work is particularly strong in its innovative use of concrete and intuitive and fluid sense of space. Later in his career, he would work for years on huge houses for very wealthy and idiosyncratic clients, like Miles Davis and Bob Hope.

The entrance to Silvertop.

SILVERTOP

Spanning seven lots off
Micheltorena is John
Lautner's "Silvertop,"
one of the architectural
highlights of Silver Lake.
Perched high on the
hill, its arcing concrete
roof can be seen from
vantage points all around
the neighborhood. It even
has a cantilevered tennis
court that is probably
the coolest place to play
tennis in Los Angeles.

95

The infinity pool with
Glendale beyond.

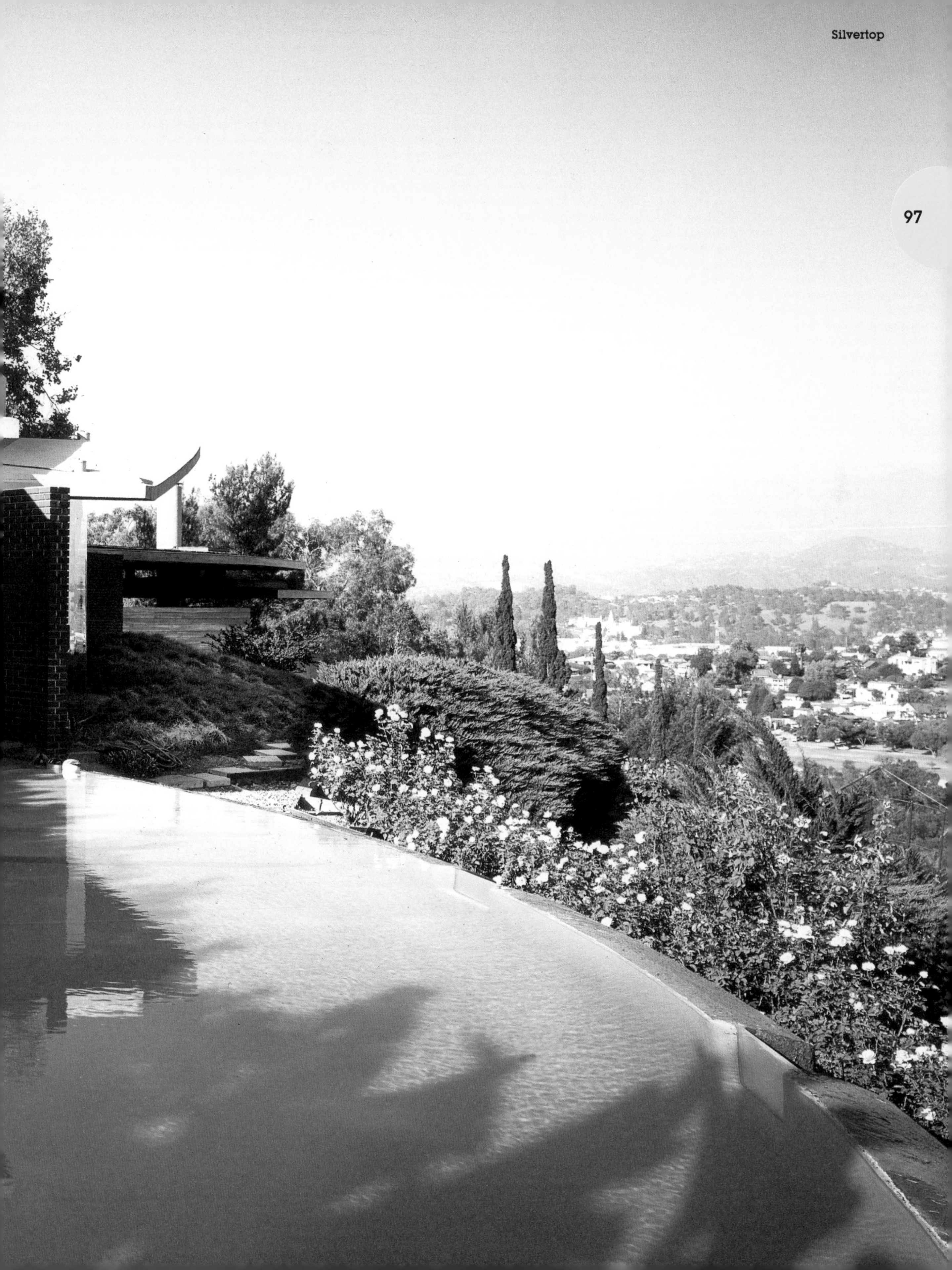

The living room is behind an arched wall of glass, which has sweeping views of Silver Lake.

100

The bathroom walls
are lined floor to ceiling
with terrazzo. In other
sections of the house,
louvered walls open
with a push of a button.

Dermott
Downs

When cinematographer Dermott D. Downs found his house in Silver Lake, it was at the end of a long hunt for something completely different. "I looked for about a year for something more mid-century and never saw anything I really liked," he says. He describes the house as a post-war stucco, *Leave it to Beaver* style home. There were plantation shutters and the house seemed dark, but it had potential.

Dermott crashed at a friend's house and lived at the Standard (hotel) while he had the house renovated. They knocked out walls, added skylights, and updated the kitchen and bath.

"My life gets so busy, I really wanted a peaceful, clean and uncluttered place to come home to," he explains. "It's really different than my old place, which had wall-to-wall folk art."

Dermott loves to throw dinner parties and there is a custom-made table in his dining room that seats a large group. The kitchen opens up into the dining room so he can socialize while he cooks. Clean, modern furniture, purchased at flea markets and refurbished, blends in with older pieces, like the folksy hutch in the dining room made by his brother that holds memorabilia and photographs. In the living room, a knock-off Mies chair has been covered in vibrant red upholstery. Next to it sits a framed poster of Dermott when he was a child actor in a KFC ad campaign. "A lot of people mistake that for pop art," he says, laughing. "My grandmother went into a KFC and had them take it off the wall for her. When she died, my mother found it rolled up in her basement."

The bathroom was designed to feel like a spa. Rough slate lines the walls, and it took two months to lay the river rocks on the bathroom floor.

The garden and outdoor living space is designed by Stephanie Bartron. The back hill is a series of terraces planted with a variety of native California plants. There is wrap-around bench seating and a fire pit around a patio that is directly off the kitchen and dining area. "My favorite thing about the backyard is the herb garden. I can just go out there with my scissors and cut what I need," he says. "I have all sorts of plans for the backyard. Eventually I want to build sort of a ghetto Neutra tea house in the back and also have a lap pool. It will make a nice little retreat."

In the corner of Dermott's living room is a framed poster of him as a child in a KFC ad.

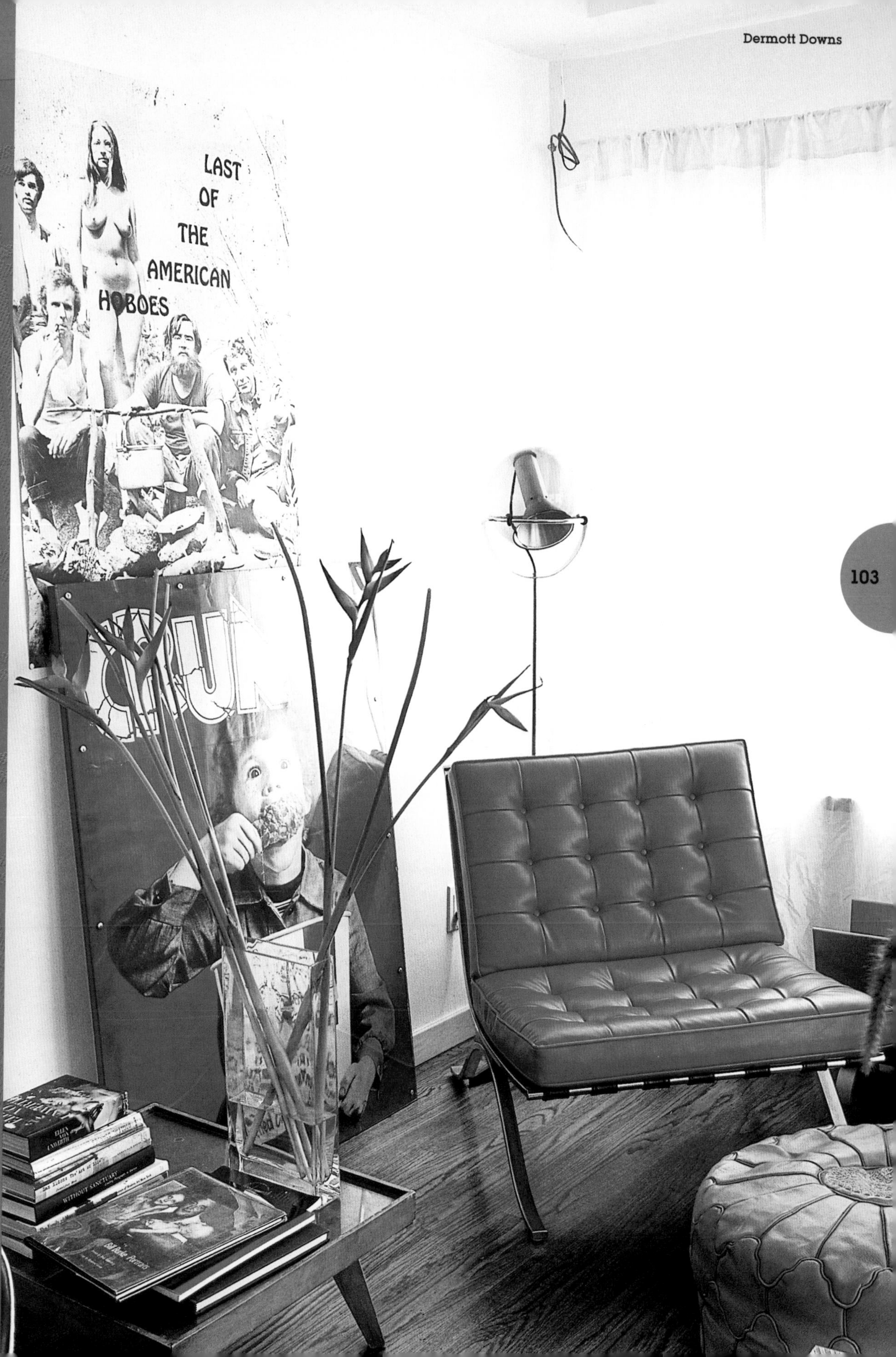
LAST
OF
THE
AMERICAN
HOBOES

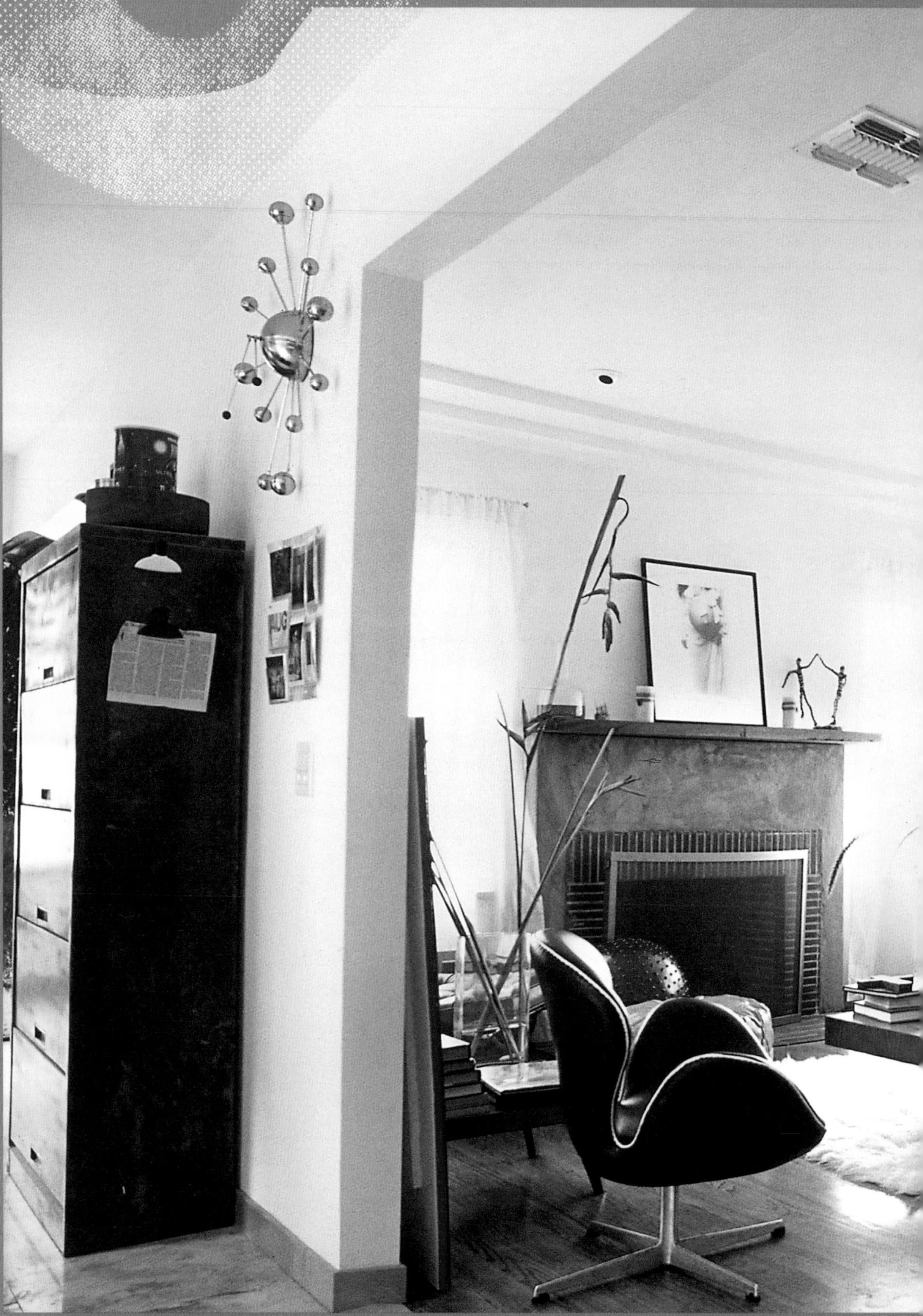

In the living room he mixes modern and eclectic, thrift store, and high art.

105

The cupboard in the corner of his dining room was made by his brother. It's where he keeps his most personal family photographs and memorabilia.

Stephanie BARTRON

Stephanie Bartron's SB Garden Design is tucked into a tiny shared office space in Atwater Village. We met not long ago when she was the office manager for the Dust Brothers' record company and a sculptor during her off hours. "I'd just finished graduate school and was trying to do the art thing while working office jobs to support myself. I realized that lifestyle wasn't working for me, so I did some soul searching and decided I should become a garden designer."

Stephanie got an apprenticeship with Judy Kameon and her firm, Elysian Landscapes, and slowly worked her way up and learned the craft. Eventually she decided to go out on her own. One of her first solo projects was designing the garden at my house in Echo Park. Since then, we have worked together on dozens of gardens, and her style has developed into something very unique.

Drawing from her background as a sculptor, her taste tends to run toward oversized sculptural plants, "especially if they look prehistoric or Dr. Seuss-like," she adds. But she is open and excited about all sorts of plants and outdoor spaces. She recently designed a garden using Australian plants, which do very well in the southern California climate. "It's nice to use these because they flourish and they aren't the plants that you see over and over again," says Stephanie. She and her husband, a photographer and writer, live in a little house in Silver Lake with their rabbits Figbash and Thelonius, and their chow-retriever mix named Lucrezia.

Stephanie Bartron's Favorite Plants:

SMALL TREES/LARGE PERENNIALS

- Angel Trumpet
- Floss Silk Tree
- Purple Hop Bus
- Myers Asparagus
- Bears Breech
- Honey Bush

VINES

- *Thunbergia mysorensis*
- Cup-of-Gold vine

BULBS/BULBLIKE PLANTS

- *Crinum* (all, but especially *cuprafolium*)
- *Tulipa clusiana*/Species tulip
- Chasmanthe

FLOWERING PERENNIALS

- Penstemons
- Salvias
- Geraniums/Cranesbill
- Lavatera/Mallow (especially the dwarf "Red Rum")
- Grasses and grass-like plants
- *Muhlenbergia dumosa*/Bamboo muhly
- *Miscanthus transmorrisonensis*
- *Carex buchananii*/Leather Leaf Sedge
- Festuca "Golden Toupee"
- Succulents
- Aloe striata
- *Agave villmoriniana*/Octopus Agave
- *Agave bracteosa*/Candelabrum Agave
- *Aeonium atropurpureum*
- *Furcraea foetida "Mediopicta"*

108

"I have all sorts of plans for
the backyard. Eventually
I want to build sort of a
ghetto-Neutra tea house in
the back and also have
a lap pool. It will make a
nice little retreat."

— Dermott Downs

Stephanie Bartron designed Dermott's outdoor area and garden space. The fire pit and wrap-around seating create additional space for entertaining.

LEFT
A desk is stacked with a
collection of books.

BELOW
A postcard advertises
their company.

JOHN + JERI HEIDEN

110

"The diversity of the artists we work with
(Madonna, Beck, William Shatner) really
reflects our own eclectic nature and taste,"
says Jeri Heiden of Smog Design. John Heiden
started the company in 1995 and his wife Jeri
joined him in 1999. Their office on Silver Lake
Boulevard has grown to employ five people
and today they have designed more than 600
album and CD covers.

Jeri remembers purchasing the house in 1991.
"We were scrambling to find a place because
we sold the house we owned in two days," says
Jeri. "John called me right away when he saw
it, wanting me to take a look before I went on
a business trip to New York. I thought it was
amazing, too."

The outdoor area is
a gathering place for
people and dogs.

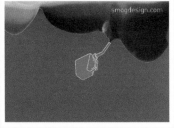

such impeccable shape that they haven't had to do any major work. There are four bathrooms in the house, all with beautiful fixtures. The kitchen has flawlessly perfect tile and original details throughout, like a great banquet and a multi-purpose kitchen desk. "The year the house was built, the kitchen was featured in *Sunset* magazine in an article called 'The Kitchen of the Future,'" she says. "I always imagine Mrs. Rule sitting at the desk, paying bills or whatever she happened to be doing." When they purchased the house, it didn't have a stove, and they searched for a mint condition 1951 O'Keefe & Merritt stove, which fit into the kitchen perfectly. "I really think the kitchen was built around that appliance," she remarks.

Downstairs, the library and den houses their collections of Eames furniture, ceramics, pottery, clocks, robots, books, and so on. "It's really John who is the avid collector. This is where we go to hang out. It's a wonderful menagerie of collections and it's a great place to look at oddities, read books, or just sit by the fireplace."

Rhodes E. Rule, an architect that worked in Los Angeles for the Unified School District, built the house in 1951. "There was definitely this institutional quality about the house that we liked," she notes. "It almost felt like an elementary school."

There is reeded glass reminiscent of a principal's office, copper doorknobs and fixtures, and built-ins throughout. "I have a feeling that Mrs. Rule wasn't quite ready for modernism," Jeri adds. There is definitely a nod toward the '40s in the house. There isn't an open floor plan—it's much more formal.

Occasionally, the Heidens will have a ceiling fixture dipped and replated, and every so often add a coat of paint, but the house is in

Their two dogs, Ripley and Jack, have the run of the house and the backyard. "They love to sit on the hill and watch the world go by," she says. "It's not a bad life."

113

114

Rick Corsini, his wife Melissa Casey, and their new baby, Lorenza, live in the Gregory Ain Apartments on Avenel Street.

Ain built the apartments in 1948 as a cooperative living experiment for a group of communists. The houses were all designed to have three bedrooms; one large master bedroom and two small bedrooms, with a sliding wooden door between them to add flexibility to the floor plan. It was actually this small group of apartments, which were independent enough to seem like houses, that inspired the high-profile Mar Vista housing tract that Ain developed later that year.

"Most of the people that originally lived here were path-breaking political types," Corsini says. Even after the communist cooperative disintegrated, progressive homeowners remained a constant—Rick recently found out that an early owner of his house was the first black man to join the Los Angeles Fire Department.

When Rick purchased the place in 1993, it was in shambles. He refers to the work he has done as "selective renovation." The kitchen is very different than the original, although it is a nod toward Ains' original plan, which included a built-in table and bench. When the house was built, the owners thought it was important to have a formal dining area, so Ain was forced to take the built-ins out of the plans. Rick remodeled the kitchen, adding that informal practicality back into the plan. "What Ain was trying to do was really considered very different, and the renovation reinforces that."

RICK CORSINI

115

ABOVE LEFT
A composite photograph
of the Ain Apartments as
they appear today.

The outdoor space at
Corsini's apartment.

Rick Corsini's living area opens into the private outdoor space, which is part of the original plan.

The entrance to the house is off a communal pathway.

117

"Most of the people that originally lived here were path-breaking political types," Corsini says. Even after the communist cooperative disintegrated, progressive homeowners remained a constant.

118

An over-sized sliding
door is used to create a
combination of privacy
and open space.

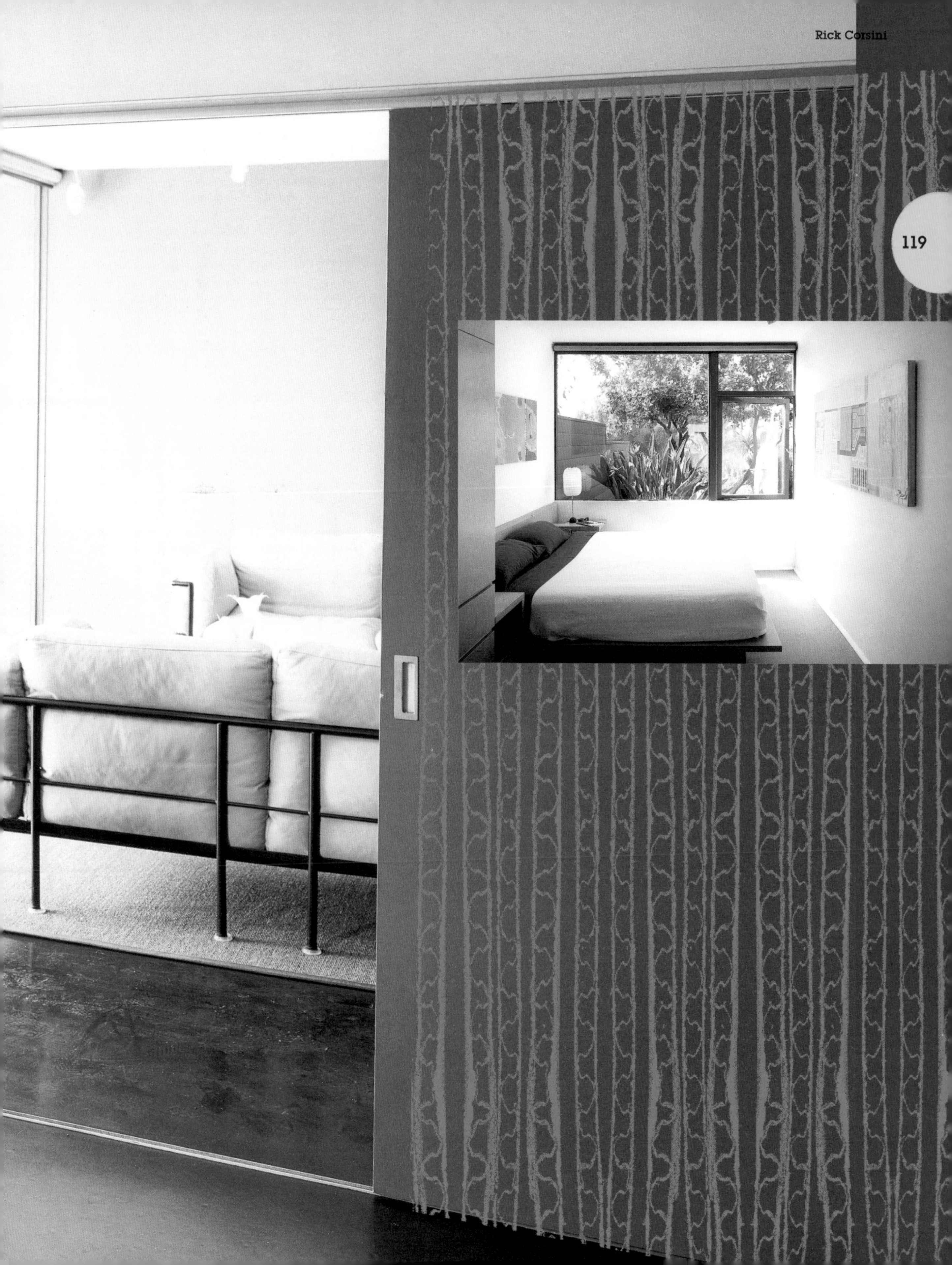

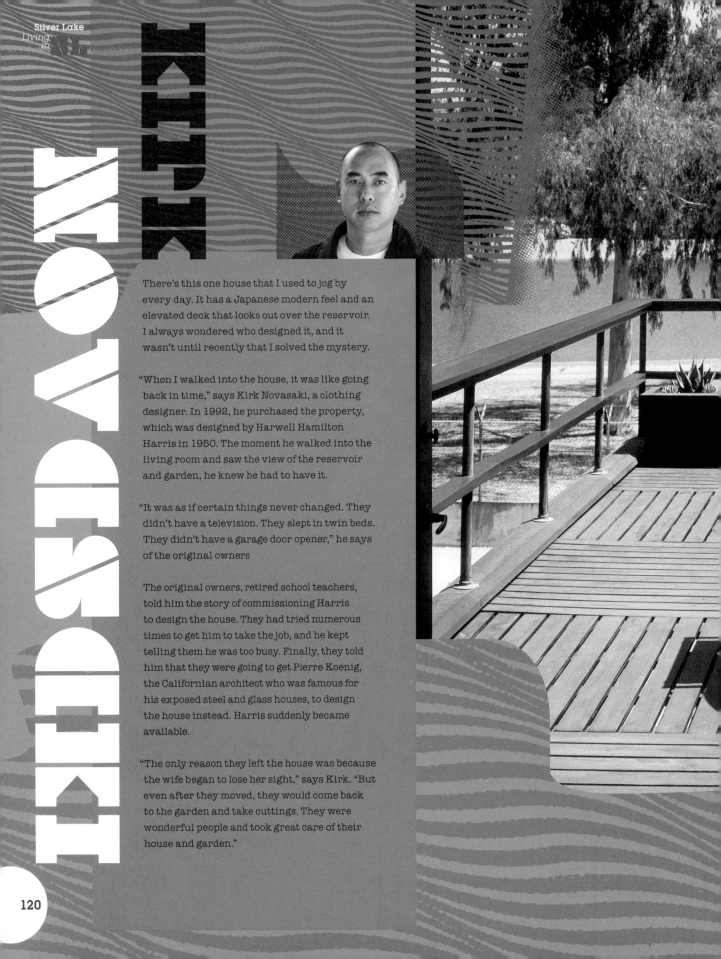

KIRK NOVASAKI

There's this one house that I used to jog by every day. It has a Japanese modern feel and an elevated deck that looks out over the reservoir. I always wondered who designed it, and it wasn't until recently that I solved the mystery.

"When I walked into the house, it was like going back in time," says Kirk Novasaki, a clothing designer. In 1992, he purchased the property, which was designed by Harwell Hamilton Harris in 1950. The moment he walked into the living room and saw the view of the reservoir and garden, he knew he had to have it.

"It was as if certain things never changed. They didn't have a television. They slept in twin beds. They didn't have a garage door opener," he says of the original owners

The original owners, retired school teachers, told him the story of commissioning Harris to design the house. They had tried numerous times to get him to take the job, and he kept telling them he was too busy. Finally, they told him that they were going to get Pierre Koenig, the Californian architect who was famous for his exposed steel and glass houses, to design the house instead. Harris suddenly became available.

"The only reason they left the house was because the wife began to lose her sight," says Kirk. "But even after they moved, they would come back to the garden and take cuttings. They were wonderful people and took great care of their house and garden."

121

The outdoor deck
makes additional
work space.

The changes he made were minor. He changed the fluorescent light in the kitchen back to the original incandescent lighting and took all the knobs off the cabinets. The original linoleum is still on the kitchen floor and so is the original Formica.

"I really like the way the kitchen is separate," he says. "There was a formality that existed back then. You cooked in the kitchen, ate in the dining room, and entertained in the living room."

The kitchen has a view of the reservoir, a detail that Harris added with the wife in mind. She had told him that she enjoyed cooking dinner, and he decided that she should have a nice view while making it.

"Living in this house is like living with art," says Kirk. Every room in the house has a view of the garden, and the architecture teases you by giving you different vantage points and scopes from every angle. "I know Harris never went to Japan, but he was clearly very influenced by Japanese design. Everything is tranquil and subtle. Things don't scream out at you."

When he moved into the house, he was so excited about the architecture that he decided to contact the owners of other Harris houses. He found a list of their addresses in the back of a book about Harris, and he sent a letter to everyone inviting them to a party. Thirty out of the thirty-two on the list responded.

"We're a very eclectic group. There's a judge, a UCLA professor, three architects, and an owner of a catering company, to name a few," says Kirk. There was a great turnout at the first meeting, and people brought plans and old photos. "We all have a great appreciation for Harwell Hamilton Harris. At the last meeting, one of the owners found the original owner who was ninety-nine years old. She came to the meeting and gave a talk. It was amazing."

The formal dining room.

"Living in this house is like living with art," says Kirk. Every room in the house has a view of the garden, and the architecture teases you by giving you different vantage points and scopes from every angle.

125

GM

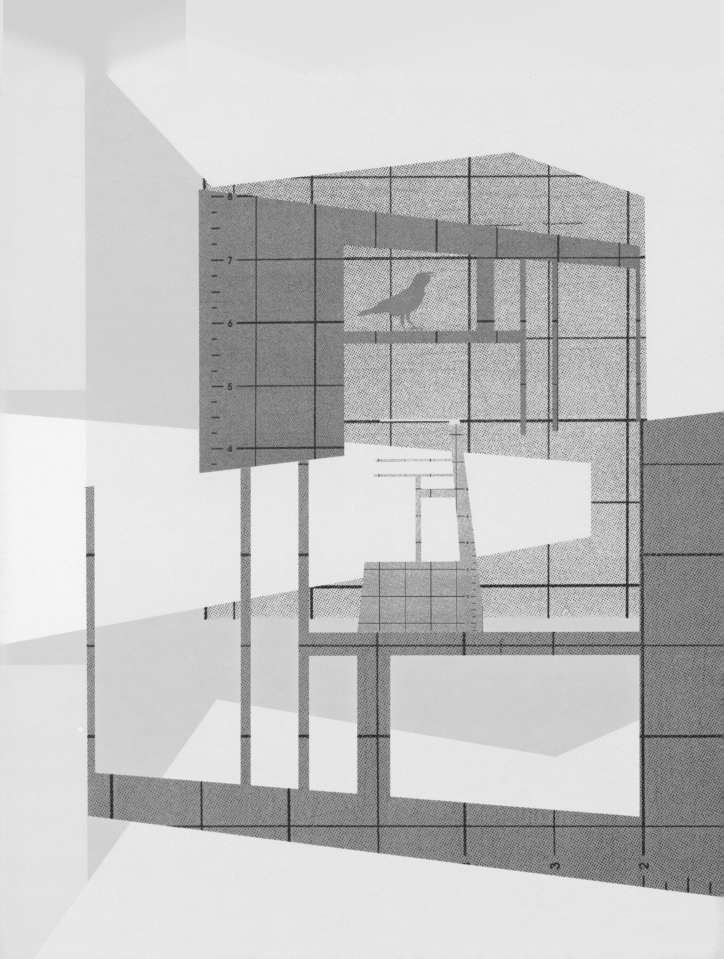

NEUTRA

Richard Neutra is L.A.'s most famous modernist architect, a practitioner of lean and mean high modernism who would paint wood columns silver to make his houses look more like steel factory buildings.

One of my favorite Neutra houses is the **VDL house** on Silver Lake Boulevard. The original burned down and was rebuilt in 1960 by Neutra and his son. The house is designed as a "machine for living": tiny bedrooms, a solarium that looks over the reservoir for tanning, and giant louvers for controlling the sunlight. At the same time, it is filled with striking optical illusions and special effects. Its most spectacular moment occurs around the entry hall, where the house disassembles before your eyes. An optical illusion is created by mirror walls and glass that gives the impression that you are looking through a glass wall into a garden with a hanging steel stair. Actually, the house is very thin at this point, and line of vision skewers straight through it to the stairs inside and the garden beyond—they are all reflected in mirrors. I call this Neutra's *Predator* effect (after the horror

movie creature), where the architecture is so reflective that it continually takes on the characteristics of the environment around it. Standing outside, a mirror will reflect the indoors, or a huge glass window will open and slide right off of the building, creating a spatial enclosure in mid air. Neutra was somewhat rigid in his geometries but wildly experimental in his efforts to expand the space of his houses into nature.

The VDL house in Silver Lake is one of Neutra's gems. It is filled with striking optical illusions and special effects.

A party at Eli Bonerz's Neutra house.

My friend Barbara Lamprecht, author of *Neutra* and *Richard Neutra—Complete Works* has interviewed many original owners of Neutra homes. She talks about the three major types of original Neutra home owners: the rich and fashionable Hollywood set of the '30s, the impoverished artists, and the progressive academic liberals—not communists, but actually quite American in their values. (Rudolf Schindler was the architect of choice for hardcore left-wing clients.) Most of these Neutra owners shared a sense of optimism for the future, and because they had hired Neutra and knew him, there was often an open dialogue about lifestyle and design choices. The Neutra houses I find most interesting are those that haven't been renovated much but have been adapted to contemporary circumstances by their second and third-generation owners.

There is a cluster of houses around the reservoir, most of them developed speculatively by Neutra. The decorating styles of the people who live in them vary from purism to mix-and-match eclecticism.

Eli Bonerz and I have known each other since I first came to Los Angeles in 1987. I ended up marrying his college roommate, Adam Silverman (see Atwater Pottery). Both Eli and Adam were trained as architects at the Rhode Island School of Design, but they veered off in a different direction when they started the "X-Large" clothing company in 1991. X-Large had some prominent partners, like Beastie Boy and businessman Mike Diamond and Kim Gordon of Sonic Youth, who fronted a spin-off company called X-Girl. We took lots of business/architecture/sight-seeing trips together to Tokyo over the years.

There are hints of X-Large all over Eli's Silver Lake Boulevard Neutra house—toys, graphics, a sticker on the fridge. He has a serious bachelor style going on—a sort of mash-up between *In Like Flint* and a vintage Herman Miller catalogue.

"I'm not a dreamer," he says, "but I thought that one day I'd eventually get a Neutra house. I had my eye on a couple along Silver Lake Boulevard and then one day there was a FOR SALE sign out in front. It turned out I was the only one who put an offer in on the house and I got it." It was 1994 and he was 26.

133

LEFT
A Marc Newson chair next to the fireplace.

The seamless line between indoors and outdoors.

134

Eli bought the house from the original owners, the Inadomis, who had commissioned Neutra to design it in 1960. "They left a lot of great things there that a seller today would factor into the cost of the house," he adds proudly. There were original plans and renderings and a custom-made, Neutra-designed dining table and set of chairs that were never manufactured.

"From what I hear, Neutra was pretty friendly with all of his clients, and he would often stop by and make suggestions on how to place your furniture, or tell you how the curtains should be hanging," he explains. "Since he was only a half block away I think he felt pretty comfortable coming over to this house."

The original owners spared no expense in upgrading the infrastructure—they added top-of-the-line copper pipes, a state-of-the-art two-zoned air conditioning unit, a prefabricated St. Charles painted steel kitchen, and plenty of high-end appliances. It was the kind of house that was impeccably maintained. "When I moved in they left me all the original pamphlets and brochures about the appliances." They also had the place covered in what was then very fashionable and expensive wallpaper. That was one of the first things Eli got rid of.

The living area boasts a
Neutra blue wall.

LEFT
A custom made Neutra-
designed dining table
and chairs which were
never manufactured.

"I wasn't trying to make this house into a museum or a period piece. A lot of people try to bring their houses back to the original style, but I'm not interested in doing that. I think as far as Neutra is concerned, staying contemporary is part of his design ideology, so I think he'd be fine with the things I've done."

Eli has a nice collection of contemporary furniture along with some older pieces. In the early nineties, there were some interesting things happening in furniture design that coincided with the price explosion of mid-century modern furniture. "Things were getting hysterical around the sale of a lot of vintage pieces, and I preferred to buy interesting contemporary stuff." Jasper Morrison, Marc Newson, and Philippe Starck are all represented.

Eli chose paint colors from the original Neutra palette—red, blue, and an extremely light yellow. On one wall there is the English version of the classic American movie poster *The Endless Summer*; beside it are some vintage X-Large posters from Japan. It all works together with the stark white pool area and a big front deck that looks out on the Silver Lake Reservoir, just down the road from Neutra's own VDL house.

The Endless Summer

137

The living, dining, and office areas all flow together and are surrounded with plate glass walls with views of the pool and the reservoir.

Outside looking in.

BELOW
The living room has a sliding glass door which goes to the outdoor living area, a speedway for trikes.

FAR RIGHT
Paul has been measured on the height chart along with all the other children who once lived in the house.

DANA BALKIN & George GRANDCHAMP

The back of the pantry door in George Grandchamp and Dana Balkin's Neutra Place home is inscribed with an old height chart, and like all the other children who have lived in this house, their son Paul Grandchamp, nearly three, has made his mark. Next in line is Joseph, who is still too horizontal to be measured.

"I loved the door when I found it," George recalls. "I didn't know much about the previous owners and suddenly I found out who lived in the house and when, how many children they had, and how tall they were." Edward J. Flavin and his wife had three sons, all of whom are represented on the back of the broom closet door.

To this day, the house is called the Flavin house in guidebooks about Neutra's architecture.

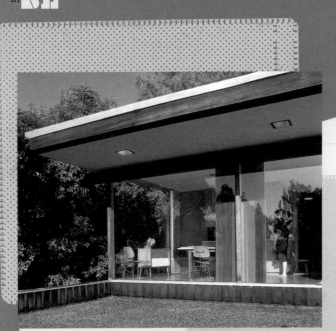

FAR LEFT
A seamless wall of glass creates an unobstructed view of the trees.

RIGHT
George's office leads the kitchen.

FAR RIGHT
John and Elysa … .

BELOW RIGHT
Original built-ins and shelves line the wall around the fireplace

The Flavins actually tried unsuccessfully to purchase a few Neutra houses before they finally gave up and commissioned him to build the house on Neutra Place. It was completed in 1957.

For George and Dana, finding the house marked the end of a very long modernist house hunt. "I remember thinking we were never going to find exactly what we were looking for," admits Dana, "but I knew the instant we saw this house that it was perfect for us."

They chose a Neutra palette of colors to add warmth. Browns and reds along with the natural woods soften the rooms. There was a lot of wear and tear on the house from the many children who had lived there, so they focused on restoring surfaces like the cork floor and chipped cabinets.

One of George's prized possessions is the cabinetry in the den and office. He happened upon a bunch of Knoll cabinets that a large office was getting rid of, purchased a truckload, and lined the walls with them and made birch tops to fit.

"I found this great old guy at Cox Paint who matched the stain to the interior of the room. I knew it was gold when I used it," he said. "That's one of the most difficult things to do when you are restoring—matching the colors and getting the tone of the stain just right."

In general, George is passionate about records and books and Dana is passionate about furniture. Most of the pieces in the house have been collected over the years or passed down by family members. There is a steel case couch that Dana picked up at a thrift store for $75, and they inherited a bunch of Eames chairs from her stepfather's office. The Nelson lamp has been in the house since it was built.

The seamless line between the interior and exterior reflects George and Dana's appreciation for indoor-outdoor living. "I love it when I'm doing something outside on the work table and Paul drags his toys out or rides his bike through the house and onto the patio. The lines are blurred," says George.

"The beautiful thing about this house is the continuity," he adds. "We love the fact that families have always lived in this house and we are carrying on that tradition. It's a wonderful space for raising kids." They enjoy the neighborhood so much that they convinced George's older son to move in just a few doors away.

CHRISTINA
KIM

I know Christina Kim, the designer and owner of Dosa (which means "sage" in Korean), from the tennis courts in Griffith Park where she practices at ungodly hours. She is at the tennis court almost every morning at 6:30 a.m. before her twelve hour workday.

It's not uncommon for Christina to travel internationally for six months out of the year. Most of her meticulously planned trips influence a line of clothing or a piece in her new home line. Despite this, Kim says it is staying home in her Silver Lake Neutra or going on long walks around the neighborhood—collecting wildflowers, leaves, rocks and butterflies—that inspires much of her work.

Her friend Larry Shafer, who lives in the other half of her Neutra duplex (and owns the fantastic design store OK on Third Street in Hollywood), marvels at her attention to the little things. "I remember we were taking a walk one afternoon and she found the most amazing pink flower. The next time I saw her, she had an entire collection of pink things in a box, all in the same hue as that little flower," he recalls. "She is an artist in her own right."

Christina Kim's clothing line hangs in the showroom along with a collection of objects and inspiration from her travels.

143

The Neutra house
Christina lives in is
calm and peaceful. She
says it is spare but not
minimal.

Much of the Dosa line—bedding, small tables, pottery—is part of Christina's home. Her style is minimal, although she dislikes that term. "I just believe that there is a lot of wonderful detail in very simple things," she explains.

A walk through her downtown loft and factory, designed by Lindon Schultz, is more like a visit to a natural history museum. Floor to ceiling windows let the sun stream into the vast space. There are tables that hold collections of natural fibers in vibrant shades, Victorian-era photographs in indigo blue tints, dusty old maps, and sketch books full of recollections from trips around the world. The clothing, housewares, and accessories that inspired her to create these objects hang gracefully throughout the space.

There are so many interesting things to see and study throughout the studio. A giant ball of mistletoe covered in khadi silk hangs from the ceiling; a stack of handmade books sits invitingly on a wooden table, each representing a year of production or a particular line.

Over the years, through traveling the world, she has forged relationships with a diverse group of craftspeople. In China, she had French lace shirts hand-painted to look like native flowers, and a visit to the Maasai in Kenya produced some beautiful beadwork. In China, Manchurian women used holographic thread to embroider a line of silk organza shirts. She also recently started a program for earthquake victims in Kutch, India. She employs more than five hundred women there to work at the traditional craft of bandhani, a tie-dyeing process.

The studio is open to the public three days a week and people are invited to linger. "I want them to have a connection to what they are purchasing," she says. "These days, it often seems like there's no connection with the *process*. I don't like it when personal assistants come in to buy. It ruins that connection. Being here in the studio brings people one step closer to that."

Jewelry, baskets, floor pillows, snap shots, vases, and teapots are displayed along with Christina's latest clothing designs.

The downtown Dosa loft gives her the space to spread out and create.

SCHINDLER

Rudolf M. Schindler is the original bohemian modernist. He was born in Vienna, Austria, in 1887 and studied architecture under Otto Wagner and Adolph Loos.

He then moved to Los Angeles in 1920 to oversee the construction of Frank Lloyd Wright's Hollyhock House, a groundbreaking concrete "textile block" project.

In his own buildings, Schindler experimented with materials, spatial organization, and construction technology for clients who ranged from modern dancers and eccentric piano teachers to Marxist political activists. Silver Lake and the Hollywood hills are alive with his low cost experiments in new ways of living.

Schindler's Oliver house is one of my favorites, both for personal reasons (lots of friends have lived there in its long tenure as a rental) and because of its stealth modernism. The house was built on Micheltorena in Silver Lake at a time when there were strict local covenants about roof types in an attempt to keep the neighborhood's semi-Spanish/ Tudor character. To that end, Schindler kept the mandated gabled roof but disguised it with parapet walls, and still managed to create a series of spaces that expand the eye outward to views on both sides of the house. At the living room level, the house forms a glass "L" around a grassy courtyard space. At the street level, the house careens away from the curb, angled across the depth of the site to maximize its spaciousness and take advantage of the natural surroundings.

These days, my friend William Doig, a designer of amazing settings for fashion photographs, lives there, and he has furnished it with an ever-changing yet minimal group of beautiful objects and furniture. Included are some original, slightly wrecked Schindler pieces that he found in the potting shed below the house when he moved in.

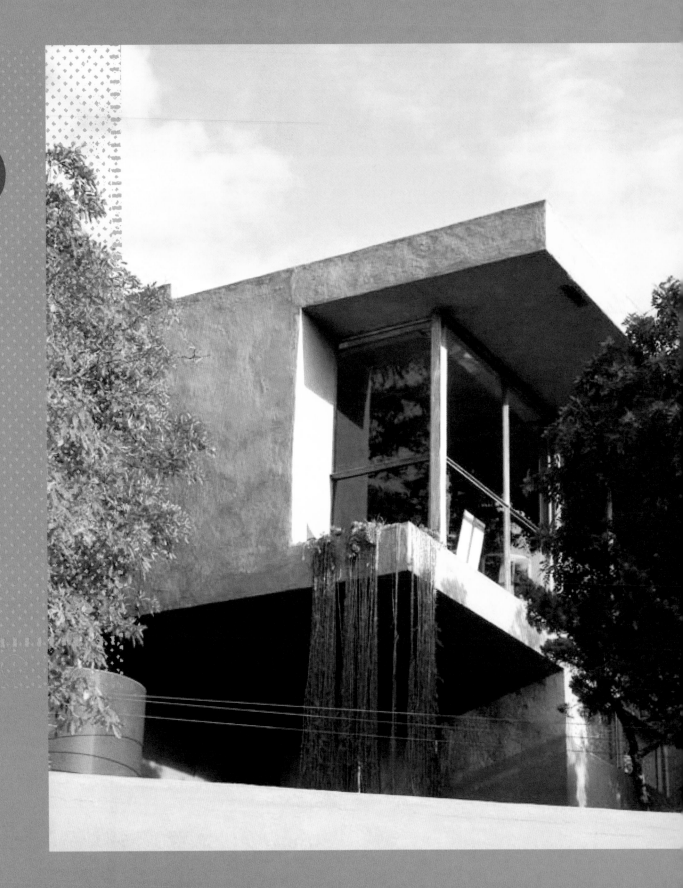

Schindler and Neutra aficionados are always
arguing over who was the better architect, and
their residential projects in the neighborhood
have become popular pilgrimage spots.
The Schindler projects are much more
individualistic—there is no idée fixe about
what they will look like as formal objects.
Rather, Schindler would work from the inside
out following his original theory of "Space
Architecture." His Howe house on Silver Ridge
sports extraordinary building technology
(board-formed concrete with wood board siding
above) and contiguous diamond floor plans.
It is one of the most beautiful buildings in
Los Angeles.

The house where he lived (now the Mak
Center) in West Hollywood is another beauty,
with a relationship between the outside and
inside (pinwheeling sections of the house
create individual room-size courtyards) so
compelling, I held my (first) wedding there.
His architecture is considered difficult to
photograph as it is so experiential and resists
easy objectification. Nonetheless, I want to
show some of his houses and apartments in the
neighborhood, as they (and their inhabitants)
provide the most direct explication of this
book's title.

In his own buildings, Schindler experimented with materials, spatial organization, and construction technology for clients who ranged from modern dancers and eccentric piano teachers to Marxist political activists. Silver Lake and the Hollywood Hills are alive with his low cost experiments in new ways of living.

A view from the interior of the Oliver house.

CONNIE BUTLER & DAVID SCHAFER

"When the Greyhound buses started to drive by, we got freaked out," says Connie Butler, a curator at the MOCA who lives in the Wilson house with her husband, artist David Schafer, and their young sons. "I think we were naïve when we bought the house and didn't realize that it was essentially like moving into a public space."

They purchased the Wilson house, which was designed by Schindler in 1938, in 1997. It was three stories with a working studio on the ground level—an artist had lived there before them. "We probably looked at it at least five times before we decided to buy it," she says. She remembers seeing the house in a real estate throwaway paper. "It was a murky little picture of a Schindler house and it had been on the market for two months, which would never happen in today's market."

Connie loves the way the light shines into the house throughout the day and at the same time loves the intimate scale of the rooms. "I think about my children growing up in this inspiring, nontraditional house, with all the glass and the view and trees, and I think it is wonderful."

That said, she is honest about the downside of the house. "This is a house with a serious agenda. It's like living in a sculpture. We really try to let scholars and architecture students come tour the house and we understand that it has a pedigree, but we haven't always liked the public aspect of living in it."

RIGHT
Judy Kameon designed a garden on a series of terraces using California natives.

Steps lead up to
different levels and
connect areas of the
house giving it a more
intimate feeling.

161

THOM ANDERSEN

My friend Amy Murphy is an architect who has done numerous mid-century renovations and is also a professor at USC. When Thom Andersen, the avant-garde filmmaker (and professor at Cal Arts), purchased the Yates house in 1996, it had been turned into a duplex and was painted a soft blue-green color. "Not what comes to mind when you think about Schindler," he comments. He enlisted Amy's help to bring the Yates house back.

The roots of the house on Micheltorena go back to 1918, when a small bungalow was built. The Yates lived there with their three sons and Mr. Yates' mother. Peter Yates was a civil servant, but on the side he wrote poetry and music criticism for *Arts and Architecture* magazine. His wife, Frances Mullen, was a pianist. They added a small performance space to their roof and hosted many of the traveling concert pianists that came to town. Schindler was commissioned to design it. The Yateses said that Schindler knew he wasn't going to make any money on it, but he had such a strong interest in supporting the arts that he did the project anyway.

> "Not what comes to mind when you think about Schindler"

An old photograph shows the bungalow on Micheltorena. Renderings of the house designed by Schindler came along and ultimately helped with the renovation and design.

The office and dining area.

RIGHT
A living space has replaced what once was the music room.

It was completed in 1938 and Peter Yates had to get seven men to bring the Steinway B. through the window to get it into the performance space. During its first year, audience members could enjoy one program for $.50 or twelve programs for $3. The series was called "Evening on the Roof," and it became so popular that they later moved it to a larger space. The series continues today with monthly performances at the Los Angeles County Museum of Art.

The performance space in the house is now a library and office, and the master bedroom is adjacent. Amy views the exterior of the house as a collage of early Schindler, late Schindler, and the existing bungalow. The bungalow part of the house was gutted and remodeled, and while the Schindler addition was completely restored, it was only lightly retouched. "I think I would have been much more intimidated by the project if it had been a high-profile Schindler house, but because it was more of an addition, it never even made it into the guidebooks," she says. "It wasn't like tackling the Howe house restoration."

The Yates library space is one of the nicest Schindler rooms I have been in—great light, a great view, and a steeply sloping ceiling that recalls a geometrically refined artist's garret.

A party at John Colter's house.

RIGHT
The living space has the signature Schindler built-ins.

SCHEINE/COLTER

SCHINDLER APARTMENT

Up the hill from my office there is a slightly weathered series of stucco and wood volumes that sprawl down the hill between two tiny streets. The Manola Court Apartment Building, better known as the Sachs Apartments, were designed by R.M. Schindler and commissioned by Herman Sachs. Sachs was a prominent artist and decorator who is probably best known for his fresco *The Spirit of Transportation* at Bullocks Wilshire and for his work as color consultant for downtown Los Angeles' Union Station. Sachs hired his friend Schindler to design the apartment complex with a penthouse and double height painting studio, and, as myth has it, with a hidden passage leading from his studio to an apartment unit in which his mistress resided. The project was built in phases from 1926 to 1940.

Schindler created the apartment building to look as though it were a part of the hillside, and he was careful to provide each unit with framed views, private outdoor space, and natural light from at least two directions in almost every room. Around the time Schindler began design work on the apartments; he wrote an essay on the natural ventilation of buildings, and the principles of natural ventilation that he explored are still at work in the Sachs Apartments.

Today, the Sachs Apartments are filled with artists, architects, and the like. Two friends of mine live there—Judith Scheine, an architect, teacher, and author and John Colter, an architect who is the senior designer in my office.

There has been a waiting list to live in the apartments since the current owners bought the building in the 1950s, and they have never had to advertise vacancies. Units are usually handed down from friend to friend. Previous tenants have included the architects Michael Rotondi, Craig Hodgetts, and Ming Fung, and the artist Amy Alpers.

Tenants often become obsessive about the building's history. Michael Rotondi has written about the building, and Judith Scheine has included passages on it in her definitive books on Schindler. When John Colter moved into his apartment he began a project that a previous tenant had started and gave up on. He is still stripping layers of paint from the kitchen's douglas fir built-in table and bench. "So much of this building is not about being pristine," says John. "It is about really living."

"One of the apartments was painted a horrible eraser pink and it's still a great space to be in, " he said. John's living space is spare, with only a small collection of modern furniture that was amassed over the years from garbage dumpsters

and tag sales. The built-in shelves in the living room are whitewashed and hold a collection of airplane parts and Campari Soda bottles. A small collection of Russell Wright ceramics lines a kitchen shelf.

Judith Scheine lives very differently, in what was originally Herman Sachs' painting studio. Her apartment is as much an office and library as it is a living space, and stacks of books and papers fill the room. It is where she has worked out the details of her research on Schindler and dreamed up some excellent buildings of her own.

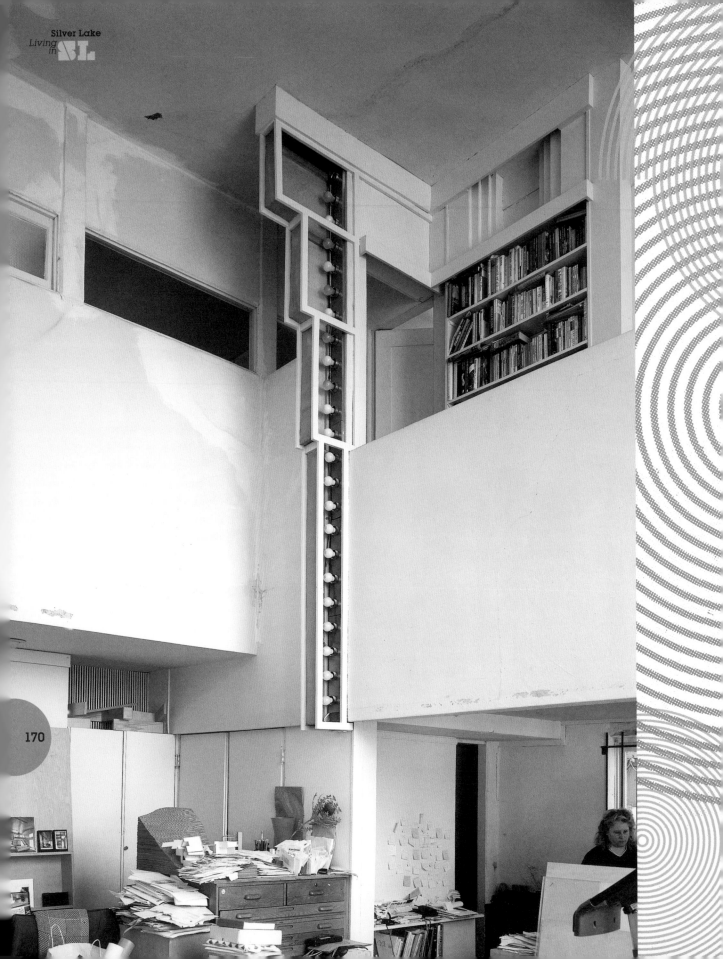

171

An overview of Judith
Scheine's office.

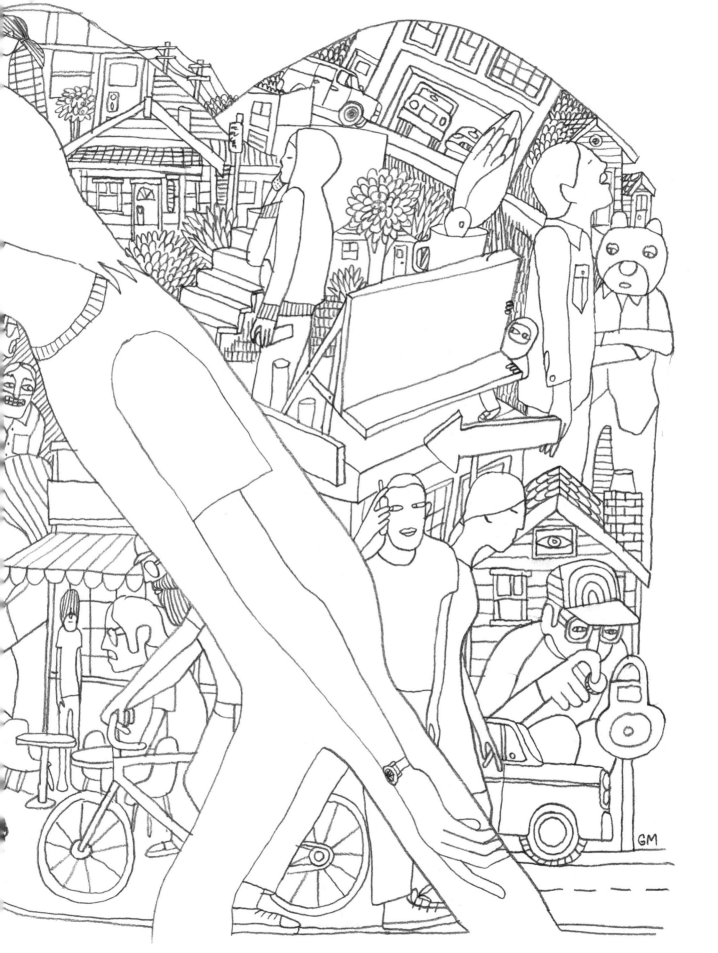

SUNSET JUNCTION

The outdoor tables at the street-side cafés are always full, and it is one of my favorite places to sit and watch artists, writers, dog walkers, fashion designers, and garage band members walk by.

Sunset Junction is the home of Silver Lake's big annual blowout—the Sunset Junction Street Fair. It is also a crossroads where some of the newer and fancier retail shops sit right across the street from stores selling leather and bondage gear. The outdoor tables at the street-side cafés are always full, and it is one of my favorite places to sit and watch artists, writers, dog walkers, fashion designers, and garage-band members walk by. So many people who live in the neighborhood are creative and many are freelance, which makes for a lively sidewalk scene any time of the day. My own office is just down the road.

My friend Wade Robinson has a design and building company called Wadeco, and he has been responsible for creating much of the look of the retail establishments along the boulevard, like the Cheese Store and the Conservatory, to name a few. He is a Silver Lake fixture and is famous for leaving his Wadeco stickers all over town. We both have daughters that attended the same schools, and our work often overlaps in the realms of construction and clients.

STELLA

Gareth Kantner has practically become the honorary mayor of Sunset Junction; he knows *everyone* and everyone comes to eat at his restaurant. A lot of people around Silver Lake credit him with the revitalization of the Junction, and shop owners admit to being handpicked to move into the retail space. He definitely had a vision.

In a previous life, Gareth was a set designer who decided he'd had enough of the movie business. He went off to Paris and, inspired by the cafés there, resolved to open his own café in Silver Lake. Café Stella, which opened its doors in 1997 as a traditional French brasserie, was an immediate success, but with only eight tables inside and ten outside, it was hard to get a seat. Eventually he bought the entire Sunset Junction, slowly expanding his café and leasing to compatible businesses like Gilly Flowers and the Cheese Store.

"We have a Silver Lake crowd," says Alain Jeu, the manager. "We have a lot of people from the neighborhood who just stroll over here, and that gives it a very European feel. There's nothing like wandering in here on a warm night and hanging out under the twinkling lights outside the café. It's almost magical."

On any given night, you'll see a diverse crowd who pop in for a glass of wine, a traditional onion soup and steak frites, or the house speciality, escargot. Escargot is one of the hottest things on the menu and people travel from all over the city to get it.

Café Stella in the evening.

Café Stella's Escargot Bourguignon

2/3 cup softened butter
1/2 cup minced parsley
4 minced shallots
3 garlic cloves, minced
1 to 2 tablespoons Pernod
Salt and pepper
24 canned snails, drained and rinsed

177

Preheat oven to 425 degrees F. Cream butter and mix in parsley, shallots, garlic and Pernod. Season to taste with salt and pepper. Pat snails dry and insert one into each shell, pushing them in as far as you can with your finger. Spoon as much herb butter into the shell as will fit. Put snails into 4 porcelain snail dishes, open ends up, and bake 10 minutes or until hot and bubbly.

Enjoy,
Alain

When Chris Pollan told people he wanted to open a cheese store in Silver Lake, nobody thought it was a good idea. "I think they thought I was ahead of the curve," he explains.

The Cheese Store of Silver Lake has been open for two years now and it has far exceeded all expectations. Pollan worked at the Beverly Hills Cheese Store for five years and always dreamt of opening his own business. He knew it was a gamble, but he had faith in Sunset Junction. "My store definitely stands on its own, but I'm lucky to have other complimentary businesses around me," he says. The store carries a variety of cheeses, including goat, cow, sheep, and blue, and a small selection of wines and gourmet items, like Del's Lemonade Mix, Little Flower Candy Co. caramels, McQuade's Chutneys, and

THE CHEESE STORE

olive and flavored oils from around the world. The French Basque cheeses and the goat's milk cheese are the store's top sellers.

On Saturdays and Sundays, he is apt to crack open a few bottles of wine and lay out a selection of cheeses for his customers. "I don't want people to feel threatened by wine and cheese. I just want them to feel relaxed and maybe learn a little at the same time."

Chris Pollan's top three pairings of wine and cheese for an impromptu dinner or party in Silver Lake:

Shasta Greenfield Cheese
a cow's milk similar to an aged Jack
Pair with a local ale

Constant Bliss
a raw cow's milk from Jasper Hill Dairy in Vermont
Pair with Schoolhouse Pinot Noir

Doddington:
a raw cow's milk, similar to aged Gouda
Pair with Robert Folley Chardonnay

Cheese, olive oil and an eclectic variety of gourmet food can be found at The Cheese Store of Silver Lake.

GILLY FLOWERS

Neal Guthrie, the owner of Gilly Flowers and Events, designs the window of his flower shop in Sunset Junction to look its best after dark. "I definitely don't design the window for the day. I like that eerie, spooky look that it has at night. It glows."

Neal likes for everything to have an autonomous, isolated look, and his choice of flowers and plants reflect that. He gravitates towards funky grasses, pods, thistles, driftwood, and anything new and different that he comes across at the flower mart. He started his business in front of the Backdoor Bakery with a couple of chairs and an umbrella, and shortly thereafter moved to the parking lot across the street. "I wanted to start something in my neighborhood so I wouldn't have to drive. I just thought, 'flowers,' " he explains.

He jumped around from space to space and most recently set up shop in the Junction. "It's so mama made. That's why I love it," he says, referring to how his business has grown over the years. Although he enjoys being an everyday florist with people who walk in off the street, he does his share of weddings and events. He particularly loves to design arrangements for architecturally significant homes in the

neighborhood. He did a giant arrangement of branches with green thistle balls for a large centerpiece at Silvertop, and he put together a desert and jungle mix for a Lloyd Wright house. "In those homes, the simplest arrangements just pop," he says. "I think an arrangement always looks its best at its purest. It goes along with the clean lines of the architecture." He likes to do the arrangements in clear glass with bark or rocks inside. "I like anything organic," he says.

Neil designs his store windows to evoke a dark eerie feeling at night.

Neil's Tips:

When in doubt, simplify. People often try to use too many flowers or too much variety. If your arrangement looks too busy, go back to one flower or a bunch of one type. And take care of your arrangement—recut the stems, change the water frequently, and keep them out of the sun.

My favorite thing to do is to comb the flower market downtown and find the craziest looking flowers, plants, vines, and weeds, and make them look wonderful. It's a great creative exercise.

Here are two examples of Gilly's signature style:

In a simple square black container:
Succulents with cyclamane
Black calalillies
Monkey tail
Fritalarea
Black tea leaf

In a bright orange square container:

Fritalarea
Cyclamane
Billy balls

181

Barbara Bestor Studio

Barbara's studio by day and by night, against some wallpaper designs developed in the studio.

183

A model of my own house from the "ReModeling" show at the Cal. State Long Beach University Art Museum.

The Silver Lake Conservatory of Music

184

On any given day, it's not uncommon to see a gaggle of young musicians warming up for a lesson at the Silver Lake Conservatory of Music. Formerly a thrift store, the space has been reconfigured and designed for the sole purpose of music instruction. There are high ceilings, low comfortable chairs placed haphazardly on an old Oriental rug, and black-and-white photographs of musicians along the two-toned green walls. The eight rooms for private instruction are cleverly named after tones in the diatonic scale.

The mission of the school, which was started by Flea of the Red Hot Chili Peppers and Keith Barry, the Dean of Education and a music instructor as well, is to provide private music instruction for young people in the community. Within a year, the school became a non-profit business, and they provide scholarships for children who are unable to afford music lessons. There is instruction offered to adults as well. "One of the coolest things I've seen are the numbers of Silver Lake families who take lessons and play together," says Keith.

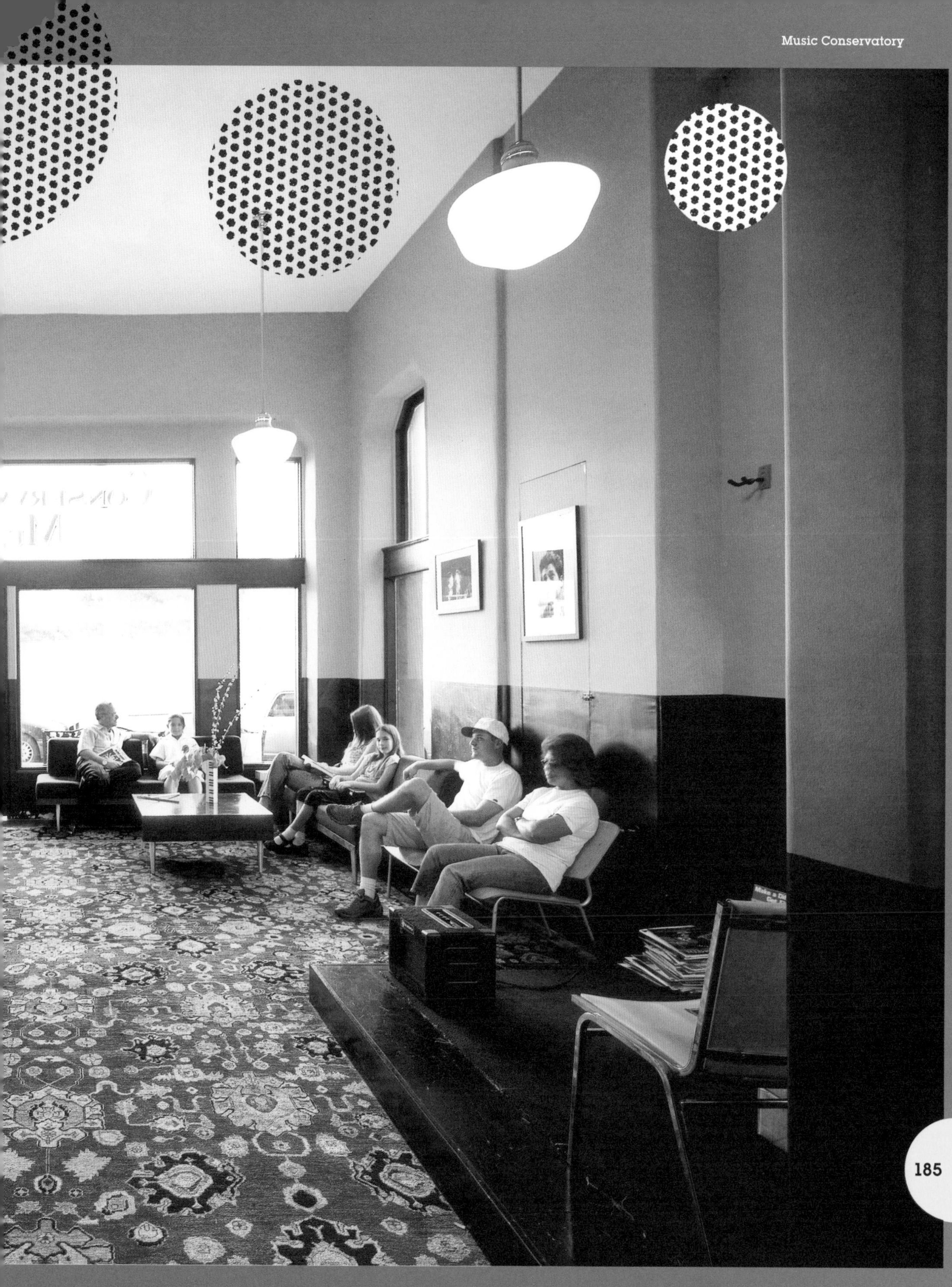

Matrushka

Matrushka Construction, once on Sunset Boulevard, is now open on Fountain and continues to host a cult following of fashionistas and politicos. Owned by Laura Howe and Beth Ann Whitaker, both artists, the avant-garde clothing boutique features one of a kind designs handmade by the owners. Inspired by the Russian constructivists, the shop is named after Russian nesting dolls. T-shirts, dresses, skirts, pants, and suits are constructed like art installations and there is almost always a nod to politics and the environment. When Howe came back after a seed collecting trip in the Sierra Nevada, she was inspired to silk screen trees on many of the pieces. Later she volunteered planting sequoia seedlings and other native plants in the Sequoia National Monument, which inspired an exhibit of artwork and silk-screens of moose, elk, and owls. The store windows always have a political message. Many of the pieces have unfinished edges which saves time on assembly and keeps the cost down, but also gives the clothing its signature "Matrushka" look.

TOP
The old shop on Sunset Boulevard.

Anyone can walk into the store, purchase an item and have it altered to fit, add pieces or trim or change buttons. They are quick to insure that there are no two pieces exactly alike and they encourage personalizing any of the pieces in the store. And they are famous for their T-shirt nights. They have an assembly line of sewers set up in the store and customers pick out pieces and patches that get sewn into a T-shirt while you wait. It usually attracts a crowd of between 250 and 350 and the line snakes around the block. When they were in the process of moving from one store to the next they hosted a T-shirt event at the Echo called Scary Politics and all the patches had a political statement on them. A favorite patch has the word "revolution" on it with helicopters and a sequoia tree. They also host art openings, which attract crowds and followers as well. Both Howe and Whitaker are passionate about keeping the clothing affordable and also educating the clientele about the inspiration. The tags on the pieces simply state "size is relative" and the shopping bags are handmade from leftover scraps.

186

MOUNTAIN Matrushka

ABOVE
Laura Howe wears her own designs.

LEFT
Beth Ann Whitaker talks with a customer. Political images and slogans are silkscreened on clothing and patches.

187

189

Inspired by the Russian
constructivists, the shop
is named after Russian
nesting dolls.

ATWATER

Atwater Village is a funny little flat neighborhood just across from Silver Lake on the other side of the L.A. River.

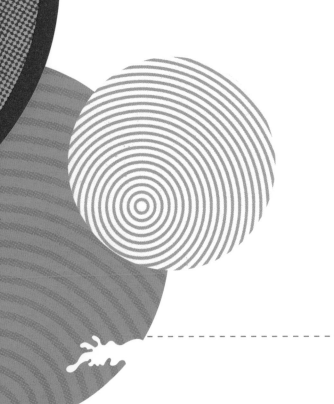

In the mid-nineties, the Beastie Boys built a recording studio there where they recorded most of *Check Your Head*. Actually, it was more accurately a recording studio/basketball court/indoor skate park/Mulberry Street style "private social club."

The two-story building they jammed this all into was a run-down retail store from the 1940s. The Beastie's Atwater–based empire soon expanded and they hired me to transform the space from a multiuse facility into a multi-multiuse facility, capable of housing both their magazine, *Grand Royal*, and record company, Grand Royal Records.

grand royal records

I overhauled the upstairs space, making it into Mike Diamond's version of a corporate headquarters. The keyword—both financially and aesthetically—was "low cost." For the interior walls and workspaces I used tilted walls made of two-by-four frames covered in homasote. For furniture I used thrift store desks tricked out in bright colors, courtesy of Earl Scheib (L.A.'s autobody-paint expert since 1937), and for the benches; diamond-patterned automotive upholstery, seen to this day in *Low Rider* magazine. It was the Fort Greene of East Los Angeles, you could say.

I eventually moved my office to Atwater and even did time on the local Chamber of Commerce. In the past few years, many other architects have been doing interesting work here—often homes for themselves or other artists. Though the real estate is no longer the bargain it once was, Atwater is still a great place to build, with plenty of flat sites and great old buildings set against the concrete-lined, industrial-romantic landscape of the L.A. River.

195

The "low cost" headquarters for Mike Diamond.

...flat sites and great old buildings set against the concrete-lined, industrial-romantic landscape of the L.A. River

RST

When I was working in Atwater, Rebecca Rudolph was a student intern who did some brilliant graphic layouts for us. Years later, Rebecca and her husband, Colin Thompson, started RST Design (Rudolph, Suarez, Thompson) with their friend Primitivo Suarez from the Southern California Institute of Architecture. They started out working together at a single computer that was set up in the bedroom of their tiny Atwater home. "It was nuts. There was no way we could work that way. Our house was only 500 square feet," Rebecca recalls. The lack of space provided the impetus for the 300-square-foot office they built in the backyard.

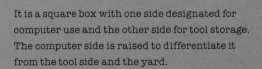

"We were definitely constrained by the size, so it was important to analyze how we all worked and used our personal space," she explains. They decided to raze their crumbling garage and build a space that would be completely separate from the house.

It is a square box with one side designated for computer use and the other side for tool storage. The computer side is raised to differentiate it from the tool side and the yard.

The simple square box design has redwood siding that has been stained a dark gray and now has a weathered look. The siding around the windows and door was turned on the vertical to create texture. Both the windows and doors are metal clad. By purchasing used flat files, Ikea table legs, and cut-to-order table tops, they got the look of custom furniture at a fraction of the cost. They put in waxed cork flooring and cantilevered stairs that float on both sides. A mini, ductless split system for heating and cooling saves space and is very efficient. The entire project cost under $35,000.

INSET
The simple square box allows all of them to work comfortably.

The redwood siding was stained a dark gray.

BELOW
The exterior of Linda Burnham's new house designed by Stan Allen.

RIGHT
Materials like aluminum, plastic, and plaster were used to build the house.

LINDA BURNHAM

"There is a real sense of space, light, and beauty in my house," says Linda Burnham. "It is very generous." I met Linda through the architects Bob Somol and Linda Pollari and was impressed by her ability to use and commission architecture as a form of self expression. It was this idea that immediately spoke to me. When I split with my husband and created a new space for me and the girls, I had to re-envision the idea of a home.

"I loved Atwater because it was off the radar," says Linda. "There were a lot of artists I knew that were working in loft spaces downtown, but we didn't want that." In 1985, she and her husband Robert Overby, who has since passed away, purchased a large 5,500-square-foot warehouse space in Atwater that once belonged to a bank. It was a mess and needed a gut renovation. In that space, which sat on a double lot, they created a small living space and two large studios (see TK architecture).

Years later, she collaborated with New York architect Stan Allen to commission a new home—next door to the warehouse but very different in feeling. This space would come to represent a separation between life and work. "I just wanted a living space with a nice bathroom, a guest room, and great light," Linda remembers.

The house turned out to be about 1,800 square feet, and full of innovative materials like aluminum, plastic, and plaster. The light and its orientation to the outdoors give it a California sensibility.

198

Linda's pet peeve is a house in which rooms aren't utilized, so she uses the whole house all the time. There is a double height living room and the guest room has pocket doors, which slice in and out of the wall. All the rooms flow into each other nicely.

"The thing I love about the house is its chameleon-like quality," she says. "It takes on the feeling of the day, and then a different feeling at night. It's much more elegant than I ever thought it would be. And since I have moved into the house, my work has become much more optimistic."

She still walks across the parking lot to her studio every day and plans to eventually build a pavilion that will link the house with the studio. But for now the separateness is welcome—this is the first time that she hasn't lived in her work studio since she was twenty.

200

She still walks across the parking lot to her studio every day and plans to eventually build a pavilion that will link the house with the studio. But for now the separateness is welcome—this is the first time that she hasn't lived in her work studio since she was twenty.

LEFT
A canopy resembling cut-out snowflakes hangs outside.

BELOW
The iT House designed by TK Architecture with graphics by Barbara Bestor.

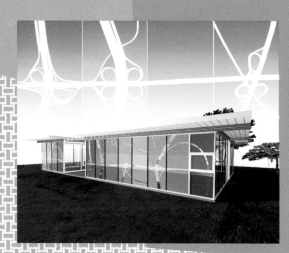

UPPER RIGHT
The interior workspace.
RIGHT
The outdoor living room.

TK architecture

A canopy that would remind you of a series of cutout paper snowflakes drapes over the parking lot at TK Architecture on Topack Street in Glendale. Linda Taalman and Alan Koch started the firm in 2003 when they relocated to Los Angeles and it is founded on the principles of speculation and experimentation. They were partners from 1993 to 2003 in OpenOffice arts and architecture collaborative and worked on high profile projects like TRESPASSING: Houses x Artists, Dia : Beacon museum, a Masterplan for Public Art and Exhibition at Ft. Lauderdale-Hollywood International Airport, public art proposals with Jessica Stockholder and Liam Gillick, and NhEW PAD.

They continue to be dedicated to speculative projects and they developed an off-the-shelf kit house—the iT house. It is made of aluminum and glass and a group of graphic artists are working with Taalman and Koch to custom design various options for aesthetics, privacy and solar control. The first iT house will be built in Orange County by art collectors John and Phyllis Kleinberg.

ADAM SILVERMAN
ATWATER POTTERY

Adam Silverman started throwing pots as a hobby, even though his first major in college was ceramics. "In the back of my mind I always wanted to be a potter," he says, "but I could never figure out how to do it."

For years while we were married, Adam was a partner at the X-Large clothing company with Eli Bonerz, his college roommate. As he became more involved in running the business and moved further away from the creative end, he realized that he needed a new artistic outlet. That's when he decided to buy a wheel and a kiln and set up in the garage. In 2001, after nine years, he decided to sell his share of X-Large and try something completely different.

His pots are high-fired and most have black stoneware bodies with his own special glazes in tones like oatmeal and soft blue. His focus is on texture. Often his pots have a luminous but archaic quality—they look as if they emerged from the earth, but the earth of a different planet.

His days are spent at his studio on a side street in Atwater, hence the name of the business. "I think my overall aesthetic has a lot to do with architecture," he says. Adam spent a lot of time traveling to Japan for business and learned a great deal about the architecture there. This summer he is going to Mashiko, the Japanese village that was the home of world-renowned potter Shoji Hamada. He also has an appreciation for mid-century Scandinavian design. "Three modern potters come to mind when I think of inspirations: the Natzlers, Hans Coper, and Lucy Rei."

BELOW
Adam Silverman in his
studio. His pots are
high-fired and he mixes
his own special glazes.

205

The house with the million dollar view.

ANGELIL GRAHAM

A house I really love in Hollywood has cheap plywood siding and a million-dollar view—it sits just beneath the famous sign on a steep hillside site. It was a personal project for architects Marc Angelil and Sarah Graham.

They recently moved their office into an equally breathtaking space—a light-manufacturing warehouse on the edge of the Los Angeles River in Atwater. It is 5,000 square feet of raw, open space, with a garden between the building and the river and a bike path in the middle. ("There's an interesting mix of bums and normal people and egrets on the banks of the river," says Sarah.) Ten employees currently work at large plywood tables that Marc and Sarah made themselves.

206

207

A light manufacturing warehouse is converted into office space.

208

209

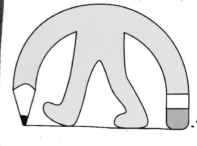

ACADIANDRIFTER

Turbo

ONE LOVE BETWEEN MAMMALS.

HOLD ON TO YOUNG IDEAS

THE SUN DOES NOT KNOW IT IS A STAR

The Solitary Arts.

210

GEOFF MCFETRIDGE

While in the process of designing this book cover, Geoff McFetridge, the graphic designer and artist, wanted to get away from the concept of a slick interior design book.

"There's a warmth that Barbara has as an architect and friend that I wanted to convey. I wanted to really take some steam out of that cliché coffee table book idea." Geoff wanted the cover to be a lighthearted illustration not only of the culture of Silver Lake, but in a larger sense, the relationship between urban Los Angeles and nature. "You'll notice on the cover that there are people walking and talking on their cell phones, but there is also nature creeping into the design everywhere."

Geoff was inspired by Richard Scarry's children's book *My House* which he has been reading to his daughter, Frances. "You can use a house to talk about life. It can create a narrative," he says. "It's about looking in through the windows and looking into people's lives. There may be a book on someone's table

that is meaningful, or an interesting flowerpot that has a story behind it."

Years ago, Geoff was working for the Beastie Boys in Atwater Village as the art director for *Grand Royal* magazine. X-Large had a gallery called "George's," curated by artist Ann Faison, and they put up Geoff's first show of silk-screened posters. "I think that's really when it all started," he says.

Geoff eventually left *Grand Royal* and got his own studio across the street in Atwater, which he's worked in for the last five years. Today his body of work is diverse—he does textiles, painting, silk screens, furniture, and character goods. X-Large, Stussy, Burton snowboards, Pepsi, Sofia Coppola, Spike Jonze, and Marc Jacobs are all clients. He says that his work style changed considerably when he got his own space. "There's lots of stuff in my studio but the walls are empty and white, and the ceilings are really high," he says. "So much of my time is spent trying to simplify my work and avoid going off on tangents. The space really helps with that."

212

Geoff McFetridge's
Atwater studio.

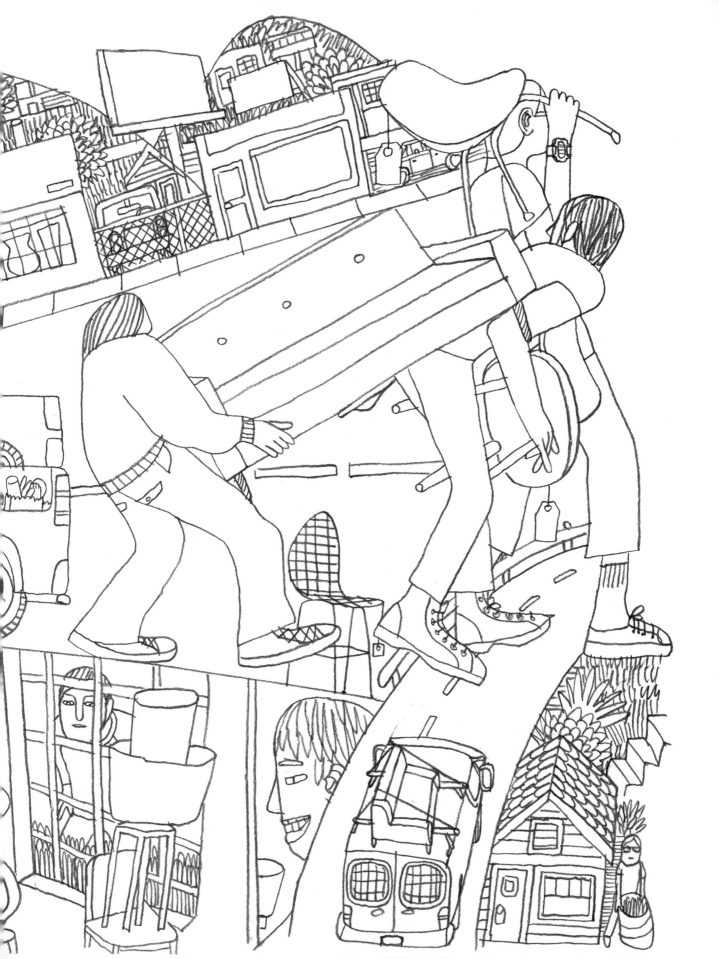

SILVER LAKE BLVD

There are too many options for eating and shopping in my neighborhood. Here, I've attempted to point out a few luminaries where the design or content makes a real difference in the quality of the experience offered.

YOLK

Just a year after finishing a furniture program at the California College of Arts and Crafts (CCAC) in San Francisco, Melanie Miller opened her own store on Silver Lake Boulevard for emerging furniture designers, called Yolk. "The name Yolk comes from the nucleus, or something that is just about to hatch," she says. The sign in the window reads, "New design is hatching all the time."

Melanie had her eye on the space, which was formerly an architecture studio, for some time, and when it became available she jumped on it and opened the store just a month later. "I called friends from art school and generally put the word out that I was looking for merchandise." Originally the store just focused on furniture, but today she has expanded into linens, home décor, art pieces, jewelry, books, and an extensive line for children—an interest that developed with the birth of her son, Oliver.

"I really try to cater to the modern parent, and there are certainly plenty in Silver Lake," she says. She carries Dwell Baby crib sheets and she also carries the Swan, a modern Swedish wooden high chair that converts to a booster seat and a chair. "Anybody who is into modern and has a child seems to buy the Swan," she says.

220

ABOVE
The exterior of Yolk on Silver Lake Boulevard.

OPPOSITE
Her own version of the rocking horse which she calls Caballo is a best-seller in the store.

As the store has grown she has begun to import a lot of pieces from Scandinavia, but she still has a commitment to local talent. One of her favorite Silver Lake designers, Byron Maes, makes one of the shop's bestsellers—a magazine rack of Formica and plywood.

"It has a fifties modern feel to it and is incredibly functional." She also sells a line of pillows from a company called PreBuild. Andy Goldman, the designer, silk screens and stitches designs onto pillows. A recent favorite of Melanie's has a pattern of yellow ducks.

Melanie's thesis at CCAC was on rocking chairs, and she features a few of her own pieces in the store. She designed a rocking lounge chair called the Yoga Lounge Chair and a series of rocking horses called Caballo, *horse* in Spanish. Today, there is a constant stream of recent grads who pass through her store trying to sell their designs. "It's annoying sometimes, but it is very difficult for me to say no," she says. "And that's really how I have found my best stuff."

OPPOSITE
A view of the entire length of the store.

The Yoga lounge chair rocks in the window.

LEFT
Tastings at Silver Lake
Wine.

Ana Henton designed
an innovative display
and storage system.

The word spread fast when Silver Lake Video closed, and there was a rumor that a new wine store might move into the space. When Silver Lake Wine opened, Ana Henton, a designer with a space directly across the street, went over and introduced herself and let the owners know that she was available for design work if they needed it. They passed, but three months later they approached her in a crisis situation because the first renovation team hadn't worked out.

The owners, George Cosette, Randy Clement, and April Langford, were on a tight budget, which forced Ana to design the space in careful phases. When they opened the store, they were selling wine out of crates and boxes. They were only able to add one design element at a time. "First we got the display cases that double as tasting spaces, then we got shelves and a desk," says Randy. "It's still a work in progress, but every time we enlist Ana, something amazing happens."

SILVER LAKE WINE

The wine shop is a high-end boutique of sorts, with a focus on small production and high quality artisanal wines from all over the world. "I had a crash course in wine," Ana says, "and I had about a month to design the space and get all the permits." She wanted to evoke the feeling of a dinner party with bottles placed comfortably along a table. The owners loved the idea and she designed three long display tables with cut-outs to hold wine bottles, and two bar-height tables, which also double as display areas. Because there was a very tight budget, everything was made of plywood. The owners wanted a comfortable, light, airy look so that people would be able to relax while tasting wine. The plywood works because it fits with the look of the wine crates.

Since the store opened, it has become a major social center. There are two or three wine tastings a week after work, and the Red Lion, a crazy old German place across the street, now finds that its booths fill up for karaoke night when the Monday wine tastings close.

In the meantime, Ana is finishing up a major remodel of a hybrid taco stand and car wash on a busy corner in Echo Park.

PHO NOODLE CAFÉ

At night if you're driving along Sunset Boulevard, Pho Noodle Café glows. There is no new signage, just a blank façade. It sits in the midst of a dingy modernist strip mall full of other tiny businesses.

Cindy Hanhdam had a vision for a late night restaurant focusing on Vietnamese home cooking—she thought it should be simple, clean, and appropriate for artists. That particular section of Sunset was perfect because it still retains the old neighborhood charm and hasn't been overdeveloped.

She hired Escher GuneWardena Architecture to design the space. "Most Asian restaurants tend to be cluttered and gaudy," she reflects. "I wanted something very simple all the way around."

The shiny stainless steel kitchen is governed by clean, minimalist lines and opens onto a long skinny dining area. The design experience carries through to details like wood grained Formica tables and the color and selection of hot sauce bottles that are perched upon each one. The lights are from Artemide and the chairs are Jasper Morrison. "We really didn't want the space to be intimidating or fancy at all, although all the materials are top quality," she says. An artist, Mathias Poledna, collaborated on the project and designed the bright yellow throwaway menus—Swiss modernism applied to a simple Vietnamese selection.

Pho Noodle Café is a late night hot spot. The Vietnamese home cooking has a cult following in Silver Lake.

PHO NOODLE CAFÉ

BÁNH XÈO

*Vietnamese Crèpe with
Lemongrass, Steak, and Shrimp*

Serves 4–6

12 oz crèpe batter *(right, number 2)*

2 lb marinated beef *(right, number 3)*

1 lb shelled shrimp *deveined, tails removed,
cooked and cut in half lengthwise*

4 cups bean sprouts *rinsed and drained*

2 cups shiitake mushrooms *thinly sliced*

1 cup mung beans *cooked*

CRÈPE BATTER

12 oz rice starch

1 tablespoon dry coconut powder

1 tablespoon curry powder

1 tablespoon turmeric

2 1/3 cup water

Use only Asian rice starch (bot gao te / bot te tinh khiet).

Combine all of the above in a large bowl and stir until very thin and slurry.

MARINATED BEEF

1 lb tenderloin beef

2 stalks of lemongrass

5 crushed garlic cloves

2 tablespoons fish sauce (nuoc mam, available in Asian specialty stores)

1 tablespoon sugar

1 tablespoon ground pepper

1 tablespoon sesame oil

1 tablespoon canola oil

2 tablespoons sesame seeds

Cut the beef crosswise against the grain into very thin slices. Discard the outer leaves and upper half of the lemongrass stalks and chop finely. Combine slices of beef with lemongrass. Add fish sauce, garlic, sugar, pepper, sesame oil, canola oil, and sesame seeds. Set aside to marinate for 30 minutes.

PREPARATION

In a frying pan, heat 2 to 3 tablespoons of oil over high heat and add marinated beef and shrimp. Cook for a few minutes while stirring.

In a nonstick pan of about 10 inches diameter, heat up to 2 tablespoons of oil over medium heat. Add 1 3/8 cup of crèpe batter mix and tilt the pan to evenly coat. Top one crèpe with 2 tablespoons of marinated beef, 6 pieces of shrimp, 3 tablespoons of bean sprouts, 1 tablespoon of mung beans and mushrooms.

Cover the pan, reduce to low heat for about 2 minutes, then remove cover. Turn the heat high again for about 1 minute. Fold the crèpe in half and put on serving plate. Repeat with remaining crèpe batter for 12 crèpes.

Serve crèpe on a plate with **accompaniments (below)** on the side. The final preparation is done individually after serving. Place a piece of the crèpe on a sheet of rice paper. Top with lettuce, cucumber, mint leaves, sour carrots and daikon. Fold and roll up, as with spring rolls. Dip in peanut sauce and eat with your fingers.

PEANUT SAUCE

1 tablespoon hoisin sauce

½ tablespoon tomato sauce

1 tablespoon warm water or chicken broth

½ tablespoon of creamy peanut butter

Combine Hoisin sauce, water, tomato sauce, and peanut butter in a small bowl and stir well to blend. Makes one serving.

ACCOMPANIMENTS

red leaf lettuce

cucumber

mint leaves

sour carrots and daikon (see below)

peanut sauce (see right)

rice paper sheets (see right)

RICE PAPER SHEETS

Place a stack of dry rice paper sheets on a plate. Cover with a damp cloth that has been wrung dry and wrap tightly with plastic film for one to two hours to soften sheets slightly. Peel sheets away individually.

SOUR CARROTS AND DAIKON

1 shredded carrot

½ shredded daikon

1 teaspoon vinegar

1 teaspoon sugar

Toss carrot and daikon in a small bowl with vinegar and sugar. Let it sit for 30 minutes. Remove sour carrot and daikon with slotted spoon and transfer to plate.

TEN 10

Scott and Joanna Nadeau have been my main suppliers, buyers, and reworkers of furniture for years and years. Just this month I bought a series of thirteen pivoting louvres from them that were salvaged from a modern office building in Colorado.

Ten ten has been Scott's lucky number for over twenty-five years, so the name of the store came naturally to him. His son's first breath was at 10:10 p.m., and it is the birthday of the well-known architectural photographer Julius Shulman (born on 10/10/10), which Scott found out during a lunch with Julius one afternoon.

For twenty-three years Scott owned a moving and storage company called Select Storage, which specialized in storing and moving fine art and high-end furniture. "I was one of those weirdos who really loved my work," he laughs. "It was through that business that I gained an appreciation for art and furniture." He eventually sold it and opened Ten 10 with his wife, Joanna. They sold mid-century modern furniture and within a year realized that they could design and sell custom couches based on old designs. "We're moving toward just selling our own pieces," he says. Currently they have four different designs and they are all made locally, and they've branched into full service interior design work as well.

It is meaningful that the business is doing well locally. Scott grew up in Atwater and had some of the same teachers that his father and older sister had. His grandfather helped build the Silver Lake Masonic Lodge, and in 1957, the year it opened, he was master of the Lodge.

Ten 10 sells an interesting mix of art and furniture and a handful of their new custom designs.

"I was raised as a part of this community. At one point I thought I would leave, but I never did. Now I'm watching all the kids I grew up with come back."

233

EDENDALE GRILL

235

"The thing I like most about the Edendale Grill is that you have blue-haired old ladies next to blue-haired kids," says Patty Peck, who recently opened the restaurant with Melanie Tusquellas in an old firehouse. For fifteen years, the building was abandoned and many different people tried to buy and make something out of it. "The city didn't make it very easy for anyone, so it sort of sat there and everyone drooled," she says.

"I finally had the opportunity to rent it from two people who were lucky enough to buy it, and I spent two years restoring it and lovingly bringing back every last lick of hardware." Edendale Grill has a community feel, and in the last few years it has become a gathering place for all sorts of people. "I have lived in Silver Lake for at least the last two decades, and the thing I love most about it is its independent, mom-and-pop spirit. You can drive for miles in Silver Lake without seeing a corporate logo."

She describes it as a place where new bohos and old bohos meet. "It has always been a politically active town with a real independent streak," she says. "I see that spirit at the Edendale, and it's amazing."

THE EDENDALE CAESAR SALAD

Edendale's Caesar Salad is a popular item on the menu, especially in the warmer summer months. We use the original recipe from the Hotel Caesar in Tijuana.

1 to 2 anchovies

1 clove garlic

½ lemon

½ tablespoon Dijon mustard

Dash of Tabasco

Small puddle of Worcestershire

Salt and pepper to taste

1 big serving spoonful of red wine vinegar

2 big serving spoonfuls of olive oil

1 cup croutons

2 big handfuls of romaine
torn into one-inch pieces

½ cup of Parmesan cheese

Start with a big deep wooden bowl, 2 forks, and 2 big serving spoons. Smash anchovies and garlic between 2 forks until they are pulverized and well integrated. Wrap a cloth napkin around the lemon half and twist and squeeze like crazy. Add Dijon, Tabasco, Worcestershire sauce, olive oil, vinegar, and salt and pepper. Mix until integrated and emulsified. Add croutons, romaine, and Parmesan. Toss vigorously and serve enthusiastically!

The Edendale Grill used to be an old firehouse.

SILVER LAKE ADJACENT

Silver Lake Adjacent includes all those other communities—Los Feliz, Mount Washington, Eaglerock, Hollywood, and Highland Park—that comprise, shall we say, the greater Silver Lake region—the five boroughs, if you will.

I try to live out most of my days within a five mile radius of my home and office, and that includes the spots where I lunch, my building projects, shopping, even my friends' houses. The following pieces all fall just inside the line and, more importantly, underscore that the bohemian modern aesthetic is not at all limited geographically to any given place.

240

CHUCK COLLINGS & TINE HAURUM + LUCY & ERIC SCHMIDT

This house in Mount
Washington was
designed in the spirit of
the Case Study houses.

Through the glass is
an amazing view of
downtown Los Angeles.

Back in 1998, my friend Michael Darling, a curator at the Museum of Contemporary Art, introduced me to Tine Haurum and Chuck Collings, an artist couple (a painter and sculptor, respectively) who needed an architect for an empty lot they had bought in Mount Washington. They had a very low budget, but they wanted to build a house for themselves and their son Oliver in the spirit of the Case Study houses that defined modernism for a generation of Los Angelinos.

We built a fairly simple box-shaped house on a steel frame that cantilevers out toward a view of downtown Los Angeles, an industrial landscape complete with Interstate 5 and the Los Angeles River. To create dimension inside the box, we stepped down one portion of the floor, increasing the height of the public living areas, and also lowered the ceiling by ten inches along the length of the rectangle. These two moves allowed for a variety of environments and a sense of enclosure within approximately 1,200 square feet of living area.

The kitchen and dining room are part of the living room but separated by the lowered ceiling, and painted a contrasting color. Much of the furniture is built-in and almost boatlike in the way it uses every inch for storage without the aid of too many closets. A special feature I am particularly fond of is the window at the dining table, which is low and reflects a narrow strip of skyline into the mirror backsplash at the kitchen counter. If you are sitting at the table with your back to the window, you can still enjoy the view in the reflection.

Other artists collaborated with us, including Monique Van Genderen, who made colorful translucent vinyl murals in the two large bathroom windows to allow the light in while allowing for privacy. The new owners of the house, Eric and Lucy Schmidt, are now finishing off some details, like a front courtyard with a fire pit and pond that were impossible under the constraints of the original budget.

TOP LEFT
The kitchen is stripped
down to the bare bones.

TOP RIGHT
The bedroom is the one
room in the house that
was virtually untouched.

AMY SIMS

For nine months, Amy Sims, an architect and a former classmate at the Southern California Institute of Architecture, looked for a mid-century modern house on the east side of town, but never really found what she was looking for. One afternoon, she walked by a house for sale in an area of Mount Washington that captured her attention. The 1922 cottage sat far back on the lot, which allowed for a great deal of privacy. In order to get to the house, which is about a third of the way back on the property, you have to walk along a meandering brick garden path. It had four major selling points: a view, a fireplace, a nice yard, and privacy.

The prior owner of thirty years had some deep-rooted privacy issues and all the windows on the 1,000 square foot cottage were nailed shut. "The first step in the process was complete deconstruction," says Amy. She painstakingly peeled the house down to its bare bones, and stripped away two layers of wall-to-wall carpeting and a layer of linoleum before reaching the hard wood floors. "I began to understand how the light worked on the site. It was during that period that I really got to know the house intimately."

"I love that this house has the feel of a tree house or a mountain cabin," she adds. There is no need for air conditioning because there are wonderful shade trees planted strategically around the house."

The main living area in the house.

In the bathroom, she will line the walls with plywood, put in a pedestal sink, and keep the old, rusted-out claw foot tub. "I want to refinish the interior of the tub and leave the rest as is for the mix. I really like the mix of found objects." She also found an old rusty chandelier in the basement which she plans to refurbish and hang over the tub.

In the kitchen, she peeled away an astonishing five layers of linoleum and plans to lay a cork floor. "I like to reuse as much as possible and use only sustainable and green products, which makes it more challenging." She plans to keep the open beams and rafters and, for budget reasons, will hang new, modern cabinets.

The only room in the house that won't be touched is the bedroom. After opening up the windows and peeling off the wallpaper, there was a nice patina left on the walls, which she plans to keep. "The trick is to keep the house's natural aesthetic, and the goal is to modernize the space."

MATT ABERLE

When Matt Aberle moved from Venice to the east side in the mid-nineties, he was looking for a perfect, pedigreed modern house. "What I began to realize," he recalls, "is that Neutras and Schindlers are amazing, but they're not really made for hanging art." Art collecting has been his all-consuming passion for some time.

Matt settled on a 1950s home, designed and built by a no-name architect, with lots of walls. He has since been collecting architects as well as art, and his next construction project is a small but bright kitchen and garage renovation by yours truly.

Thirty-six year old Matt traces his love of collecting back to baseball cards as a kid, and eventually punk rock records as a teenager. "I spent a lot of the eighties buying seven-inch singles and spending time in the record swap meet scene." He still houses a collection of vinyl in his office.

He got involved in the music business, and when he started to make money, he started buying art. His visual sensibilities were honed by his mother, a fashion designer who spent time taking him to all the exhibits at local museums and galleries. "Whether it was King Tut or contemporary, she always brought us to see art," he says.

His first piece was an Uta Barth photograph from the ACME Gallery in 1994, which he purchased for $1,500. "I remember how nervous I was about buying it and how much time I took to make that decision," he says. It took him six months to pay it off in installments.

His collection has grown and evolved since then, and he has been lucky enough to maintain relationships with artists and dealers his age. "Those were the people that I could afford to buy when I started," he explains. He has always been supportive of Los Angeles based artists and his timing was perfect—just as he started to discover work that he wanted to buy and collect, the Los Angeles art scene exploded. There are many pieces that he purchased years ago that he would be unable to touch at this point. "It's intensely gratifying when you choose to buy art that you love and suddenly curators are interested in that particular artist—all of a sudden, they're on the map. And when the artist grows, you grow too."

Often it is the personal relationships with the artists that make a piece particularly special. One of Matt's favorite pieces is a tiny flower painting by Takashi Murakami. When he

Matt Aberle's gallery space that houses his art collection.

purchased the painting, Takashi told him that he had worked on it for two years and signed it twice. In the corner of the painting there is a tiny blob of white paint—a purposeful mistake to show that there is always imperfection. "It is a deliberate gesture to show that Takashi made this piece himself and that's why I love it so much," he says. He also loves a recent Elizabeth Peyton painting that is a copy of a Da Vinci from the National Gallery in London. The unusual historical painting hangs in his bedroom. "It's the last thing I look at before I go to bed and the first thing I look at in the morning when I wake up."

Matt's post and beam house is also a great canvas for his collection of mid-century modern furniture. His two favorite places to buy furniture in Los Angeles are Skank World and AK11/14. Over the years, he has collected pieces like his George Nelson coconut chair and Milo Bausman baseball chair, and even though the house is full, he keeps buying. "If I see a chair I love, I'm very apt to pick it up," he admits. And the furniture collection has certainly helped him in the art buying arena. "I traded an Eames 670 rosewood chair and ottoman for a painting that I just had to have."

As the collection grew, he began to put pieces in storage, trying to figure out new and different ways and places to hang art in his house. It was when he purchased his Laura Owens monkey painting, which is about ten feet by six feet, that he knew he needed to build an addition. "That is one of my favorite pieces, but I had no walls large enough to hang it," he remembers. He put a call into a friend who suggested architect Mike Ferguson, and they went to work designing a space for more art. "I basically told him that I needed a room with a lot of wall space, and I let him do what he wanted."

Ferguson added onto the back of the house in an area that was essentially a dirt basement. A floating staircase connects the house with the room, which boasts twelve-foot ceilings and very little glass. The room is sparse—it is mainly just a place for the art. There is a shockingly red Dosa rug on the floor, which he feels is in keeping with his aesthetic. "I spend a lot of time in the space just looking at the art or watching TV," he says. "It's a really pleasant place to spend time."

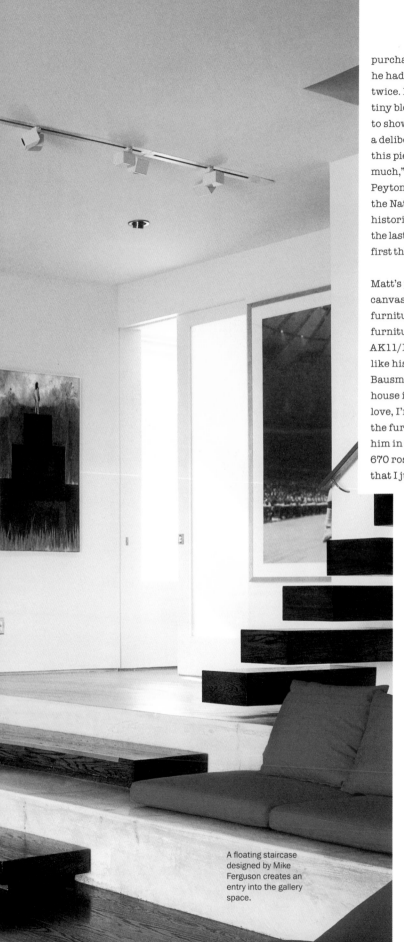

A floating staircase designed by Mike Ferguson creates an entry into the gallery space.

LEFT
Lost and Found is a series of little store fronts that connect. From boots to jewelry to house wares, to art, she wants her customers to connect with what they are buying.

I grew up in a world of bookstores, modern furniture, moms in batik-screened halter tops and super graphics. I felt pretty comfortable when I first went into Jamie Rosenthal's row of stores off Hollywood Boulevard. "When I look around my stores I often think about Cambridge, Massachusetts, in the '70s. Those memories have impacted all different parts of my life today, most importantly my aesthetic," says Jamie Rosenthal, owner of four amazing shops just outside the Silver Lake city limits called Lost and Found. "I wanted my store to evoke the same heady combination of intellect and design I felt when I walked into a childhood friend's house."

Jamie sells silk-screen prints, dishes from Finland, crafts from Africa, clothing from small independent designers, and jewelry from local artists, just to name a few of her eclectic offerings. "As a child, I thought that every kid grew up with a copy of *The Family of Man*, Marimekko, and artifacts from world travels," she laughs. Her major influences as a renegade retailer are progressive, liberal values and the ground-breaking modernist retail emporium Design Research in Cambridge.

Jamie opened her first shop, a children's store, about six years ago. The space was located in a rough area without a lot of other retail space, but the shop had worn hardwood floors and

LOST and FOUND

high ceilings, which was enough. She set out
to fill a void that she noticed in retail around
Los Angeles. "I wanted to shift away from blind,
meaningless consumption and create a place
where people could come and connect."

The children's space soon had a cult following
and it became a destination. The second
space expanded on the concept and carries
art books, home goods, furniture, women's
clothing, and great design from all over the
world. She describes the second store as "the
world according to me." The final two spaces are
considerably smaller and she refers to them as
her social laboratories. One space sells shoes
and accessories and the other, her favorite, is an
art supply store combined with a gallery.

"I am most proud of the art store because I
believe it's the most original," she says. It has
the feeling of entering an artist's studio. There
are books about typography on the shelves,
artists' works on the wall, supplies to create
with, and even a photo booth. Jamie hopes
that shoppers will come in to buy, and walk out
inspired to create their own art.

She is quick to point out that the spaces are in
constant flux, so there is always something
new to see. "I wanted these spaces to raise
awareness and help people create a comfort
level in their own homes," she said. "I like to
think that the things I sell have soul."

"I wanted my store to evoke the same heady combination of intellectual and aesthetics design I felt when I walked into childhood friends' houses in 1970s Cambridge, Massachusetts."

BLACK SHEEP KNITTERY

Black Sheep Knittery is in a tiny sliver of a space stocked to the gills with amazing yarn.

Opening a knitting store always felt like a daydream for Kristel Moffett, owner of the Black Sheep Knittery. The long skinny space shares the block with Lost and Found, and in a similar fashion has created a destination and community for local knitters.

Formerly a movie publicist, Kristel quit her job when she got pregnant with her daughter and decided to be a stay-at-home mom for eight years. Eventually, she caught the knitting bug and had the idea of opening a store. Jamie Rosenthal of Lost and Found would call her every time a retail space opened up on the block, and finally the time seemed right.

Kristel carried hand-dyed wool, exquisite silk yarn, and a variety of other high-end products from small, independent yarn businesses and good old-fashioned yarn companies. Every week there are a variety of classes and workshops. "I've found that people are desperate to create things, and knitting is a very unassuming outlet for creativity," she says. "It's super meditative and attracts an incredibly diverse crowd."

255

GEOFF McFETRIAGE & SARAH DIVINCENTIS

When Geoff McFetridge (see Atwater) and his wife Sarah DiVincentis got married, he designed a poster to be their wedding invitation. "It was a picture of a house with all sorts of elements that our friends would recognize, like my crazy hybrid stereo."

Geoff and Sarah's ideas about a house were fairly simple. They weren't looking for a "name" architect. When they went house hunting, they were thrilled to find a ranch. "I've always loved ranch style houses and they are harder to find over here," Geoff says.

The house was built in 1953, and it went up for sale when the original owner passed away. "It was a wreck. It was carpeted and wall-papered to death." They cleaned it up and painted it, and had me redo the bathrooms. "We're not really furniture collectors," he admits. "We just like having a house that you don't have to worry about."

He still does all his silkscreen work on the kitchen table and he doesn't have to worry too much about ink spilling or getting paint anywhere. "I like to think of it as comfortable-creative; and it's good for our daughter, Frances, too."

Barbara designed a simple bathroom for their house.

258

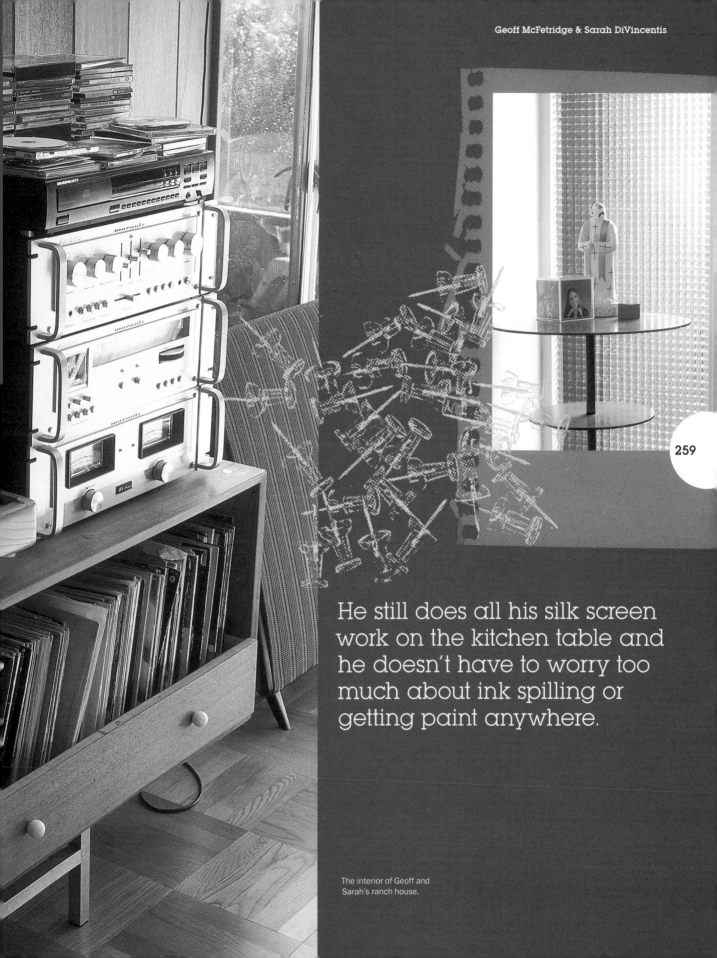

259

He still does all his silk screen work on the kitchen table and he doesn't have to worry too much about ink spilling or getting paint anywhere.

The interior of Geoff and Sarah's ranch house.

Acknowledgments

This book would never ever have been conceived without Judith Regan's encouragement and enthusiasm! I would like to thank all of the friends and family who helped the endeavor along. Specifically: Annemarie Bestor, Claudia Bestor, Jon Huck, Susan Morrison, Paul Simms, Nicolai Ouroussoff, Jessica Marshall, Paula Norman, Rebecca Hughes and Deirdre Mendoza. I would especially like to thank Kim Stevens, Josh White, Jon Huck (again), Geoff McFetridge, Michael Worthington and Simon Storey without whose amazing work the book would still be just a nice idea. The people I work with have provided much love and support and helped design and build our projects that appear in these pages: Elinor Nissley, Selena Linkous, Alice Park, Talbot McLanahan, Monte Ross, Anne Porter, Mark Skiles, Laurent Turin, Celia Miller Parker, Catherine Johnson, Thea Massouh, Scott Mitchell, Mary Ruppenthal, Rebecca Rudolph, Pete Fanello, Ben Harrison, Henry Gordon and Jessica Pregnalato. I would also like to thank my early clients who took a chance on experimental modernism and got Bestor Architecture rolling: Pat and Maiya Verrone, Ed and Cynthia Solomon, Chuck Collings, Tine Haurum, Tina Carter and Josh Oreck, Mike Diamond, Natalie Hill, Adam Silverman, Eli Bonerz and Eddie Cruz. My mentors/friends/colleagues in the architecture racket: Dagmar Richter, Norman Millar, Roger Sherman, John Dutton, Marc Angelil, Robert Somol, Ann Bergren, Andrew Zago, Robert Mangurian and Mary-Ann Ray have all set the bar very high. The Los Angeles Forum for Architecture and Urban Design has kept all of our hopes and dreams for progressive architecture alive and the Southern California Institute of Architecture with its incredible faculty and energy has changed the built environment of our city for the better.

Additional Art and Photograph Credits:

Art Center College of Design: page 88; Beatrice Bestor: page 13; Claudia Bestor: pages x, 16–17, 224; Marina Chavez: pages 8, 9; Doug Hill: pages vii, 1, 3, 70–71, 154, 183, 194–95; Ray Kachatorian: pages vi, 10–15, 18–19; Erich Koyama: page 163; Selena Linkous: page 24; Thea Massouh: page 114; Amy Murphy: pages 163–65; Erik Otsea: pages ix, 43–44, 159; K.C. Perry: page 18; Anne Porter: pages 182–83; Nancy Steiner: pages 8–9; Simon Storey: pages 28, 34, 37, 48, 80, 84, 86, 111, 115–17, 133, 136, 160–61, 182–83, 186, 197, 203, 208–9; The Architecture & Design Collection—University Art Museum, UC Santa Barbara: page 136; TK Architecture: page 203; Hilary Walsh: pages 7–9, 16, 42, 45–47, 131, 141, 166, 178, 179; Jeremy Williams: pages 182–83.

BOHEMIAN MODERN